Happy Birthday Lori

♡ Stephanie

Ordinary WALKS WITH AN Extraordinary GOD

FIFTY-TWO DEVOTIONS TO KEEP YOU IN STEP

ROBYN RISON CHAPMAN

WESTBOW
PRESS®
A DIVISION OF THOMAS NELSON
& ZONDERVAN

WestBow Press books may be ordered through booksellers or by contacting:

WestBow Press
A Division of Thomas Nelson & Zondervan
1663 Liberty Drive
Bloomington, IN 47403
www.westbowpress.com
844-714-3454

The cover photo features a sunrise and a glimpse of my childhood home on "The Ridge."

ISBN: 978-1-6642-5196-0 (sc)
ISBN: 978-1-6642-5197-7 (hc)
ISBN: 978-1-6642-5209-7 (e)

Library of Congress Control Number: 2021924887

Print information available on the last page.

WestBow Press rev. date: 12/14/2021

CONTENTS

FALL

WINTER

Acknowledgements

Thank You, Jesus, for Your love and forgiveness. My hope is in You alone.

To my best people, Derek, Jack, and Max, I love you. Thank you for allowing me the space to make this happen. I'm glad I get to do life with you people.

To Kristin, thank you for being anything I needed you to be through this process, especially tech support and a friend at all times. I love you.

To Susan, thank you for the idea, the push, and for always believing in me. I love you.

To Kelli, thank you for your listening ear, your prayers, and your light when I was in the dark. I love you.

To my editor, Kay Pflueger, thank you for making sense out of my rambling thoughts. This is infinitely better because of your thoughtful, caring work.

Thank you, dear reader, for going on this journey with me.

INTRODUCTION

From Genesis to Revelation, scripture is full of references to walking. God walked with Adam and Eve in the Garden of Eden. Enoch walked with God. Noah walked with God. We walk by faith and not by sight. We are told to walk humbly with our God, to walk in the light, to walk in love, to walk in the law, to walk through the valley of the shadow of death, to walk in a manner worthy of our calling. Revelation tells us we will one day walk in white.

This devotional is the result of walking humbly with our God. For several years, I have been walking almost daily. It began as a simple, safe exercise for my bad knees. It grew into much more than simple exercise. It did help me lose weight and become healthier. But it has done so much more. It has helped to clear my head and my heart. It has boosted my soul in a way that I didn't see coming.

I usually walk between three and five miles six days a week. There's nothing sacred about the distance. It's just that I have the routes measured, and since I was aiming for forty-five minutes of daily exercise, I found three miles takes me just about that long. Over time, those ordinary walks have evolved into forty-five minutes of uninterrupted time with our extraordinary God. It has been lifesaving in ways that I'll never fully be able to explain.

I have walked my way to better physical, mental, emotional, and spiritual health. I have learned some priceless lessons on the nearness of God and just how active He is in the smallest details of our lives if we allow Him to be.

Though I have been a writer for my entire adult life and a Christian even longer, I never considered writing a devotional until God began stirring my heart during a season of grief. What began as a conversation with friends turned into a blog, and later, an idea for a devotional. Simply put, this work is the result. God asked, and I have tried to obey.

My prayer is that you will find hope, encouragement, perspective, and, most of all, God in these pages. I am no theologian, Bible scholar, or best-selling author. I am simply a grateful Christian who is learning to seek and find God in every day. I want to share this with you, friend, in the hope that you will seek and find Him wherever your road leads and in all the seasons of your life.

May we all walk humbly with our God one step at a time.

Blessings,
Robyn

Spring

HOPE OF SPRING

AND A GREAT WINDSTORM AROSE, AND THE WAVES BEAT
INTO THE BOAT, SO THAT IT WAS ALREADY FILLING. BUT
HE WAS IN THE STERN, ASLEEP ON A PILLOW. AND THEY
AWOKE HIM AND SAID TO HIM, "TEACHER, DO YOU NOT
CARE THAT WE ARE PERISHING?"

—MARK 4:37–38

I love spring. It has for a long time been my favorite season. Its arrival means we've made it through another winter.

When I was a kid, spring always reminded me that it was time for baseball. These days, it's more about hope. I enjoy the contrast of winter into spring. My walks help me notice that the blooms on flowering trees are the prettiest, most vibrant color when the sky is gray.

The contrast is vivid. I like the definition of contrast—"strikingly different from something else." It reminds me of Jesus calming the storm. You can find this in the Gospels of Matthew, Mark, and Luke. Jesus and His disciples were in a boat crossing the lake, and Jesus was asleep. A storm was raging. The boat was filling with water. Disciples were panicking.

Talk about strikingly different! Jesus slept while they were terrified for their lives. They woke Him up, and He rebuked the wind and the waves. He questioned their lack of faith. I probably would've struggled with faith as well. Fear is powerful, especially when you have so little control over the circumstances, but Jesus is more powerful.

We can choose to focus on either side of the contrast. It's like Peter walking on water to Jesus. He was fine when he focused on Jesus. When he took his eyes off Jesus, he began to sink. If we focus on the storm, it pulls us down. If we focus on Christ, we can keep going.

There are plenty of storms in the world to frighten us all. That just means the contrast is all the better. Living through a pandemic gave us plenty of opportunities to choose where to look. It was not hard to focus on our loss of normal. It was right in front of our faces. Basic needs became apparent. Fear was real.

It was easy to see the needs and darkness. We can focus on that, or we can focus on the hope that comes when people step up and help. It's focusing on Jesus in the middle of the storm. Times of darkness create opportunities for us to be hope, to share hope, and to see hope if we choose to. The greater the need, the greater the opportunity. The worse the winter is, the more hope spring provides.

We can focus on the storm and on the people who choose to look down as Peter did, or we can focus on the people and situations that are showcasing the best of humanity. We can look for those people who are showing kindness and loving their neighbors. If you don't see one, be one. Stay focused on the hope. Keep your eyes on Jesus and on the people behaving like Him.

Spring reminds us to do that. Life and color and warmth come back. It brings Easter, when Jesus gave us the ultimate hope and proved that no storm, not even death, lasts forever. All of us must go through winters and times of raging storms, but exactly none of us have to stay there. Spring is an annual testament to that.

Action: Deliberately spend time looking for Jesus in your current storm.

WHEN IT DOESN'T MAKE SENSE

So the last will be first, and the first last. For
many are called, but few chosen.

—Matthew 20:16

I was walking on an absolutely beautiful yet unseasonably cold day in early May. The sun was shining. The sky was bright blue. Everything was colorful and blooming. I wanted sunshine and blue sky, but I might have traded both for warmth. Then I noticed a tiny little cloud. It seemed lost, but maybe it just showed up to deliver this message.

A bit of science here. Clouds are strange in that they can both keep temperatures warm and also cool down the temperature. The absence of clouds sometimes will allow for a cooler temperature, while cloud cover can keep the warmth.

The thought of clouds helping to keep a warmer temperature is counterintuitive to me. This led me down a road of things that don't make sense. And I realized that God often works in ways that seem illogical to me.

I think about biblical examples of people who were not necessarily qualified for what God called them to do—Noah, Abraham and Sarah, Moses, David, Ruth, Mary, Paul. They didn't make sense from a human perspective. How many of us have felt unqualified for the task God gave us?

I have experienced my offerings to God, both money and time, come back to me in ways I couldn't otherwise explain. It simply doesn't make sense. The Bible says, "The last will be first," and "Turn the other cheek." These are concepts that don't always make sense to us. God has a track record for turning suffering into something that glorifies Him and blesses us. What looks tragic to human eyes can be a catalyst for amazing blessings.

I've taught multiple Sunday school lessons on Romans 5:3–4, which tells us that trials ultimately produce hope. We have put that to the test through a pandemic. This might be the closest we will ever get to actually stopping time. I spent far more time with my husband and kids than in our normal life, where we wouldn't see one another nearly as much. There's suffering involved when we can't work and live as normal, but it has absolutely produced perseverance, character, and hope in our house. It doesn't make sense, but we received time. It's the only thing we can't get more of.

God will use suffering that doesn't make sense for His glory, and that works out well for those who trust in Him. We can have faith while we build our hope. Philippians 4:6–7 says God's peace surpasses all understanding. It won't make sense to our human minds, and it doesn't need to. What an amazing gift that makes no earthly sense. We are not going to understand all the whys and hows. God's ways are seldom going to make sense to us, and they don't have to. We just keep trusting Him even when it seems to make no sense.

Action: Think of an experience where God showed up or blessed you when it didn't make sense.

Mix It Up

Have I not commanded you? Be strong and of good
courage; do not be afraid, nor be dismayed, for the
Lord your God is with you wherever you go.

—Joshua 1:9

I always take the same route on my morning walks. Same direction every time. I'm a creature of habit and enjoy the comfort of the routine. Plus, it allows my brain to focus on other things and not on where I'm walking. If my body is on autopilot, then my brain is free to pray, listen, and think.

Because of some high water one day, part of my normal route was closed off. I was forced to go a different direction. It was only a small portion of the road that was blocked, so I walked in a backward direction all the way around to it from the other side and then back, like a pendulum instead of a circle.

That was strange even though it was the same neighborhood where I always walk. I saw all kinds of things from the other side. There was a large RV parked on the side of a house that I didn't even realize was there. I saw the house from the other side and learned something.

God doesn't want us to miss out on opportunities to grow and see life from another direction just because we're comfortable in our routine. Getting out of our comfort zones is how we learn. It's how we make new connections. It's how we can bring glory to Him. It forces us to trust Him.

It's hard to voluntarily leave our comfort zones. Sometimes we can do it; other times, God literally blocks our path and forces us to go a different way. God pushed me out of my comfort zone by asking me to stop working and to spend more time at home, focusing on my family and writing for Him. That might sound wonderful to some, but it is out of my comfort zone. Giving up an income was a big step too.

Those changes in my life's direction forced me to trust and grow closer to Him. It made me think of Joshua as He began to lead the Israelites after Moses died. Moses is an obvious example of God pushing someone out of his comfort zone, but I can't help but wonder how Joshua felt. He had the job of finishing what someone else started. Was he out of his comfort zone? Was it a job he felt ready and prepared to do?

Imagine if God dropped that in your lap. Joshua knew the stakes. He knew the battles that awaited. The Promised Land wasn't unoccupied. He knew what God had promised if the Israelites could be faithful. As much as they questioned Moses, it's easy to see how one could be skeptical of them holding up their end. I wonder if that's why the Lord repeatedly told Joshua to be strong and courageous.

Don't be surprised if God forces you to change direction and sends you out of your comfort zone with a command to be strong and courageous. When He does that, He also does it with a promise to go with you.

Action: If God is changing your direction, let Him.

CHASING PAVEMENTS

BUT SEEK FIRST THE KINGDOM OF GOD AND HIS
RIGHTEOUSNESS, AND ALL THESE THINGS SHALL BE ADDED
TO YOU.

—MATTHEW 6:33

God sure has a good sense of humor. I started a walk by turning my music on shuffle. The first song that played was "Chasing Pavements" by Adele. I laughed about it for a minute, and then God made it clear there was a lesson to be learned.

The song is about a romantic relationship, of course, but the lyrics, "Should I give up or should I just keep chasing pavements? Even if they go nowhere," can apply to so many things. Most of us are chasing dreams, callings, and goals of some kind—romantic relationships, friendships, careers, and various hobbies and achievements. It's hard to know whether to give up or keep going.

Writing often feels like I am chasing pavements. I spend a lot of time and effort thoughtfully crafting messages God has put on my heart and ones I believe have value for many of us who are just trying to keep our heads above water. Today's world of technology means I share most of that work online. It often feels like people pay no attention to my words. However, if I make a mistake or fail at something, it seems like everyone notices. Those lyrics play on repeat in my head. Should I keep chasing pavements even if it goes nowhere? If no one reads what I write, if no one responds in a way that makes me aware of it, should I keep writing?

Yes. I should. And you should, too, friend. If God has put something on your heart to do, then do it. Do it for Him even if it feels like it's going nowhere. If He told you to chase something, then keep chasing it with all your soul. It won't be for nothing.

Let me pause here to highlight the fine print of Matthew 6:33. We need to be seeking God and His kingdom first. If whatever you're pursing trumps that, stop immediately. When we pursue Him first, He takes care of the rest.

If my pursuit of writing gets in the way of my pursuit of God, then I'm doing it wrong. If your pursuit of a spouse, a child, a career, a lifestyle, or an achievement is getting in the way of your pursuit of God, then you need to pause and adjust. Now, if you are pursing God first, seeking His will, and the gifts and dreams He has given you are consistently leading to Him, then keep going with all you have. Keep chasing that pavement.

It will lead somewhere even if it doesn't seem like it all the time. It will lead to the peace that passes all understanding. It will lead to you seeing just how faithful, even in the tiniest details, God is. It will lead to God being glorified. It will lead to eternal rewards.

Action: Evaluate what you're chasing. Does it lead you closer to God? Does it point others to God? Does it require the use of skills He already gave you? If you answered yes, then keep going.

THE DEVIL WON'T COME LOOKING LIKE A BAD GUY

I was walking one morning after a substantial rain. Puddles were everywhere, and dead frogs were scattered around. Wait ... what? Yes, dead frogs. Could've been toads—close enough. Actually, squashed frogs would be more accurate. Just stay with me here.

Frogs and toads come out after heavy rains to mate and lay eggs and because they need a dark, wet environment. They need conditions that don't dry them out. If you were a frog, that day looked good, as it was exactly what you needed (except for the frogs that got squashed). They hopped to the road, and bad things happened. That day, I passed four squashed frogs.

First, gross. Second, I got to thinking about how those poor frogs didn't know what hit them. Satan comes at us this same way. He doesn't show up with a pitchfork and horns. It's easier to run the other way when the bad guy looks bad. You don't have to tell me twice. I'm out.

Here's the thing though. Satan is good at being bad. He's a crafty one. He doesn't show up in our lives looking like sin and trouble. He shows up looking like just what we need. If we fall for that, we're going to get squashed like those frogs.

Satan masquerades as an angel of light (2 Corinthians 11:14). He comes at us in disguise, looking like the answer. He looks like the light, but his motive is clear. He wants nothing more than to destroy us. We must stay alert. He's prowling around, looking like what we need. Like the rest we crave when it's time to work. Like a friend who will get us into trouble when loneliness is haunting us. Like birthday cake when our health is suffering. Like a plausible excuse to get us out of something we don't want to do.

We're not unaware or ignorant of Satan's schemes (2 Corinthians 2:11). He is actively trying to trip us up, especially as we grow closer to God. He doesn't need to spend time hunting for those he already has. He comes hard after those who are obeying God.

So, what can we do? Be aware. Be vigilant. The Bible (1 Corinthians 14:33) says God is not a God of disorder but of peace. This is a real clue when we're wondering if something or someone is from God or the devil. Chaos and disorder don't come from God. God doesn't try to confuse us.

We're not always going to get it right and know when it's Satan. He's not going to wear a name tag. It helps to know God. As scripture says, His sheep know His voice. The more we know Him, the better we can distinguish what is from Him. Study his Word and pray. Seek guidance from a pastor or trusted Christian friends.

White noise is prevalent. Lots of people claim to have answers. Be careful, as the devil is real. Do not let your guard down.

Action: Make it a point to learn God's voice.

Purpose in the Rock

And He said to me, "My grace is sufficient for you, for My strength is made perfect in weakness." Therefore most gladly I will rather boast in my infirmities, that the power of Christ may rest upon me.

—2 Corinthians 12:9

Have you ever tried to walk with a rock in your shoe? I have, and I discovered that little things like that make a big difference. It only seems to happen when I'm on my daily walks and am wearing expensive shoes intended for that purpose—not on a quick trip to the mailbox wearing flip-flops.

I wonder why this happens. My shoes fit, and I'm wearing them properly. What dawned on me is that it happens when my shoes begin to wear out. That particular pair, about six months old, had logged four hundred miles, which is on target for when they need to be replaced.

So, when a high-end pair of walking shoes begins to wear out from doing exactly what they are made to do, little things begin to cause problems. Oh yeah, I feel a lesson here.

I never stop to take the rock out. I don't want to stop for two reasons: One, it is awkward on the side of the road. Two, I like to race myself and reach my time goals. I try to ignore it and shake it to one side. However, I have realized, no matter how small, when something not supposed to be there gets inside, it takes over. It distracts. It causes pain. It can make me want to quit.

Just like life. When we get worn down, even from doing what we were made for and what is good for us, something little can cause pain and discomfort. It can alter our focus and make us want to throw in the towel.

We can kick it to the side for a while, practice mind-over-matter skills, even use it as motivation. Eventually, though, we must deal with it. It makes me think of Paul's thorn in the flesh (2 Corinthians 12:7–10).

We don't know for sure what that thorn was. It doesn't matter *what*. It matters *why*. That *why* was so Paul and others would know of Christ's power; so Paul wouldn't become conceited and stop relying on God; so people wouldn't give too much credit to Paul; to show that in all things God is enough. *Why* was to show us that sometimes we must complete the race with a rock in our shoe.

We all deal with things that torment us—sin that trips us up, challenging personalities in our path, health problems, financial troubles, circumstances that don't seem to improve. Sometimes those rocks are the first indicator that something needs work. Something is wearing out and might need some TLC. If you've done what you can, asked God to fix it, and His answer was no, maybe He's got a bigger *why* for you too.

We might need the reminder that God's grace is sufficient. He might be doing something big through you and needs to humble you. Take it to God before giving up.

Sometimes a fresh pair of shoes does the trick. Sometimes God removes the thorn. But sometimes His answer is "My grace is sufficient for you." Are you ready for that answer?

Action: Ask God to remove your thorns, but be prepared if He doesn't.

PUDDLES

DO NOT BE DECEIVED: "EVIL COMPANY CORRUPTS GOOD HABITS."

—1 CORINTHIANS 15:33

One of my post-rain walks meant walking where there were a lot of puddles. A car passed through one of them, and I got a healthy splash. It was just like a scene from a movie where the innocent bystander gets splashed when the bus drives through the puddle. I feel like you all should know that and get a laugh. I certainly did. Just know that if you're going to walk in the road after rain, you'd better be ready to get splashed.

As I continued to walk, I noticed puddles under trees were rippling like it was still raining. Those puddles were too close to the tree limbs and were catching all the drips. I felt that when I was splashed—just too close to the water.

Does it seem like you're always being splashed by life? Pay attention to where you are, what you're doing, and who you're spending time with. Friends, we might be getting wet just because of where we're standing. Think about that.

I write a lot about topics such as hope, faith, grace, and love, but that's not all there is. Sometimes we need to be reminded that the wage of sin is death (Romans 6:23). Sin is not to be toyed with. I often tell my children how easy it is to be guilty by association. We must be careful about where we're standing. The edge of sin is a slippery slope. You might be flirting too heavily with temptation.

I think about how Lot chose to move closer to the corrupt, sin-filled city of Sodom. He could have chosen a different direction. It was like pitching his tent right at the edge of sin, and it didn't end well.

I think about Samson flirting around with Delilah about the source of his power. I am sure he thought he could handle it—that he could stop before he said too much. But he couldn't, and it cost him. The Lord left him, and the Philistines gouged out his eyes.

How many times have we been guilty of trying to walk up to the edge of sin, expecting to stop just short of it? Many times, we ask questions about where the lines and boundaries are, just to see how close we can get without crossing over them. The problem with this mentality is that you don't have to be standing right in the puddle to get wet.

If we keep toying with sin and walking near the edge of the puddle, we will get splashed. If we're hanging out with people we shouldn't, standing in places we shouldn't be, or if we're relying on our own strength to stop before it goes too far, we're going to suffer. There will be consequences that we don't want to face.

Friends, sin is not worth the risk. It is not something to play with. Don't go where you know trouble will be. It's far easier not to go than to try to leave once you're already there.

God offers help in temptation. Take it before it's too late.

Action: Take an honest assessment of your situation. Are you consistently getting splashed? Move away from the edge of the puddles.

FATIGUE CRACKS OF PARENTING

REJOICE ALWAYS, PRAY CONTINUALLY, GIVE THANKS IN
ALL CIRCUMSTANCES; FOR THIS IS GOD'S WILL FOR YOU IN
CHRIST JESUS.

—1 THESSALONIANS 5:16–18

I've noticed cracks in the road that I walk on. This is what is referred to as *fatigue cracking*—these interconnected cracks that occur under repeated traffic. It happens because the road is doing what it's supposed to do. Occasionally, there can be a structural flaw, but most often this is simply what happens over time. The cracks allow moisture infiltration, and it can deteriorate into the dreaded pothole.

Ah … fatigue cracking. I feel that in my soul when it comes to parenting. I'm just doing the best I can, trying to survive, and then boom, fatigue cracks begin to show. Not a pothole but definite cracks.

My kids seem to take turns having rough stretches. It feels like it's always one of them. I should be thankful they both don't hit at the same time, but it feels like a never-ending battle. Thus, the fatigue. And then cracks begin showing.

I do not feel good about that. Children have been caught making bad decisions, lying to cover tracks, backtalking, and a *lot* of complaining about the consequences. Thus, I am fatigue cracking all over the place.

God is clear that in parenting and Christian life, discipline is a must. I know. The Bible tells us to train up a child in the way he should go, and when he is old, he will not depart from it (Proverbs 22:6). Discipline is painful at the time but later produces a harvest of righteousness and peace (Hebrews 12:11).

However, as much as I love to look forward to the promises of God, my fatigue cracking is happening today. I reread verses like Colossians 3:21, "Fathers, do not embitter your children, or they will become discouraged," and then I get discouraged. Have I gone too far and discouraged them? Did I discipline the appropriate amount? Did I break his spirit? Fatigue cracking.

I must repair this cracking before the devil gets in and creates a pothole. And we all know how long and hard it is to get a pothole fixed. God pointed me to 1 Thessalonians 5:16–18, and I pondered it a while. "Pray continually," I read.

In the middle of my frustrations, I can pray. When I am worried that I've gone too far or not far enough, I can pray. When I want to cry, I can pray. This doesn't mean I have to take to my knees in my closet. In fact, parents of young children, please don't leave them unsupervised. Just whispering the name of Jesus is enough. He hears us.

Give thanks in all circumstances. God was anticipating these moments of frustration and cracking when He said *all* circumstances. I can be thankful for the opportunity to fix these issues before they become bigger issues. I can be thankful when my kids act their ages. I can be thankful for that little human who still hugs me and says, "I love you, Mommy." Giving thanks is an elixir that cures a multitude of issues.

Fellow fatigued parents, inhale, exhale, whisper a prayer, give thanks, keep going. Your work is important and will be rewarded.

Action: Take a deep breath. Pray for your children.

Prepare Your Heart

"Let not your heart be troubled; you believe in
God, believe also in Me."

—John 14:1

It is strange to me how God chooses to drop something onto my
heart. Walking up a hill one day, I wondered why I was doing it …
the hill, I mean. I was not preparing for a race. I didn't have a goal
contingent on hills. I was just preparing myself to keep going. I do like
to be prepared, but for what?

I couldn't stop thinking about what we're preparing for. Marathons,
retirement, vacation, weather, next week? Do we have emergency kits
full of batteries and nonperishable food? Do we have enough toilet
paper? If 2020 taught us anything, it was that many people highly value
having a stockpile of toilet paper.

I'm making light of it because it highlights the point that when push
comes to shove, you can see what people place value on. Or how quickly
we turn to panic. This made me think about the end of the world. I
don't remember a time when people weren't convinced that Jesus was
returning any day now. Wars, disasters, plagues, pestilence, questionable
leaders, these are not new to the world. We are. Many people believe we
are in the last days. Perhaps we are. I don't know.

It's preparation I'm thinking about. Jesus talked about his return in
Matthew 24. He told His disciples not to be troubled. He said no one
knows the day or the hour, but we are to be vigilant and watchful.

If you believe it's time, what are you doing about it? Are you preparing as Jesus wants us to prepare or by panicking, stockpiling, or maybe doing nothing? I am preparing for heaven, not doomsday. I'm not saying you shouldn't save or plan for how to function in an emergency. I am saying if you believe Jesus is coming back, prepare your heart and encourage others. Now.

In John 9:4, Jesus said, "I must work the works of Him who sent Me while it is day; the night is coming when no one can work."

There's no need for panic. Urgency but not panic. Make sure your heart is right with the Lord. Ecclesiastes 3:11 tells us that God set eternity in our hearts. If we want eternity in heaven, we prepare our hearts now by accepting Jesus and sharing Him with others. Peter (1 Peter 3:15) told the early Christians to always be ready to give a defense for our hope. That is preparation worth doing.

Being prepared for the return of Jesus isn't about how much we've stockpiled or a physical battle to wage. It's knowing Him and how much of His love we can give away.

In 2 Peter 3:10–13, we're told the day of the Lord will come like a thief in the night. If we are living godly lives, we can look forward to this day. However, if you don't know Jesus, you'll know doom.

I have no idea about the end of all time, but our time is near. If we're more concerned about a storm than eternity, we have work to do. If we value toilet paper above souls, our preparation is misguided. It is time to prepare your heart.

Action: Give your heart to Jesus. If you have, share Him with others.

Renew Your Strength

My brethren, count it all joy when you fall into various trials, knowing that the testing of your faith produces patience. But let patience have its perfect work, that you may be perfect and complete, lacking nothing.

—James 1:2–4

I had fallen out of the habit of doing push-ups before going on my walk each day. As I began again, I noticed that doing them seemed harder. Using a muscle strengthens it, and my muscles were struggling, as I hadn't been using them consistently. It was noticeable!

I wondered how many other places in my life I had let the muscles deteriorate. If we've been neglecting an area, it weakens. Relationships and skills are the same. They must be worked regularly. That doesn't mean we've lost the skill or that we can't get back to levels we once were, but if we don't use it, we are going to lose some ability.

Our spiritual life is the same. If we don't attend church, pray, read the Bible, or spend time with God regularly, our spiritual life will deteriorate too. If I have not been doing those things like I should, dealing with the junk that Satan throws at me becomes heavier very quickly. I become out of shape in those areas.

Exercising our faith can be tricky. How's your faith in God right now? Just like our muscles, we can tell if our faith has been exercised regularly. Really exercised, not just given lip service. In today's world, it seems like everyone's faith is being tested simultaneously. We can expect our faith to be tested.

Fear seems easy to spot. It shows up in news stories, conspiracy theories, loneliness, job loss—just to name a few. Do your faith muscles know God is still there? Ephesians 6 describes the armor of God. It says the shield of faith is our protection. You're going to have to develop the muscle to use it.

Have you been exercising your faith muscles? You know when you are just going through the motions as compared to doing the heavy, consistent lifting that strengthens us. I'm reminded of Isaiah 40:31, which says, "But those who wait on the Lord shall renew their strength; They shall mount up with wings like eagles, They shall run and not be weary, They shall walk and not faint." When we put our faith in God and do what He asks of us, our spiritual muscles strengthen.

I pray you are strengthening your faith instead of succumbing to fear. Let's use this as an opportunity to see where the work is needed before it's too late. Simply put, it's hard for us to hold up when life gets heavy if we've let our faith muscles get weak.

If you've got areas of life that aren't holding up, chances are you've not been working those muscles.

Action: Is fear getting the best of you? Check your faith. Exercise spiritually areas where you feel weak.

In the Details

"Look at the birds of the air, for they neither sow
nor reap nor gather into barns; yet your heavenly
Father feeds them. Are you not of more value than
they?"

—Matthew 6:26

I had been busy with breakfast for the kids, packing lunches, verifying the day's schedule, reminding them to fix their hair, brush their teeth, put that book in your backpack, and just answering all their vastly different, rapid-fire questions.

In the middle of that "get ready for school" chaos, I paused to finish my coffee. I opened social media and saw the lyrics to "His Eye Is on the Sparrow" and then heard the song "How Great Thou Art" in the next post. It brought tears to my eyes. Such calm certainty in the middle of the noise and swirling activity.

After I got the family out the door, I went out for my daily walk. As I walked, I noticed the sun highlighting a heart-shaped leaf and the grass covered in dew drops. Friends, God loves you enough to be in the smallest details of your life. My thoughts went to the verses in Matthew chapter 6 about not worrying. When Jesus was describing why we shouldn't worry, He was pointing out just how involved in the small details God is.

His words tell us that if God provides food for birds, helps the lilies and the grass grow, He will certainly take care of His children and their needs. News flash, friends, as one of His children, my needs are not just for the major things. I need to survive the morning chaos every day. I need to find the lost item, remember who has a game today, check on my people, get the stain out of the shirt, get the oil changed in the van, pay that bill, figure out what to fix for dinner, and so on.

Our daily grind doesn't always include the big miracle. Not every day is the day your life changes direction. Most days are not about grizzly bears. They're about mosquitoes. They are mustard seeds. And God is just as active in those nuggets of your life as He is in all the big things.

Look throughout scripture at how God was in the little details. God made armies smaller. He used a child to kill a giant with a rock. He was in a still, small voice. He used a child's meager meal to feed thousands. He sent Jesus as a baby. God is in the small things, and He values the tiniest details.

Nothing is too big or too small for God to handle. He wants you to take all your requests to Him. Don't make your relationship with Him just about life's major events. Give Him your everyday details. Then be prepared for Him to show up in your morning chaos to remind you that His eye is on the sparrow and He watches over you. Don't be surprised when He uses the sunshine as a spotlight on a heart-shaped leaf, and all you can think about is how much He loves you.

Action: God is very much in the small details of your life every day. Look around. Note where you've seen Him today.

Think about Good Things

FINALLY, BRETHREN, WHATEVER THINGS ARE TRUE,
WHATEVER THINGS ARE NOBLE, WHATEVER THINGS ARE
JUST, WHATEVER THINGS ARE PURE, WHATEVER THINGS
ARE LOVELY, WHATEVER THINGS ARE OF GOOD REPORT,
IF THERE IS ANY VIRTUE AND IF THERE IS ANYTHING
PRAISEWORTHY—MEDIATE ON THESE THINGS.

—PHILIPPIANS 4:8

Today as I walked my usual neighborhood route, my mind bounced from thought to thought—about chores I needed to get done, the challenges I struggle with as a wife and parent (especially parenting—this is a bottomless pit), whether or not I am doing enough and committing enough time and resources to all the things I supposed to, and even to the state of the world. It makes for a heavy walk when my mind begins to run away like that.

It may feel as if the world is burning down around us with so much bad news, so many problems, and so many unanswered questions. Anxiety tugs hard when we go down that road in our thoughts.

When my thoughts outpace me like that, I try to collect myself by asking Jesus to change my thinking. Not a deep, closet-type prayer, just a "Jesus, help my thoughts" prayer. Praying forces my mind off worldly things and back to Him. It's a reset for my mind. Sometimes it needs to be reset every few minutes. Other times, it lasts a little longer.

On this day, He reminded me of Philippians 4:8, which tells us to meditate on things that are true, noble, just, pure, lovely, of good report, virtuous, and praiseworthy. That completely changed the rest of my walk that day. I began to look for things that struck me as being pretty. I made a mental list of things I know to be true, starting with the fact that Jesus loves me.

Some translations of this verse say, "Fix your thoughts." Meditate means to think deeply or focus your mind on something for a period. If we're fixing or meditating, then we need to spend some time with these thoughts. We need to dwell on them.

Friend, do you ever give yourself a few minutes to just think about lovely things? You should. I should. We don't always need to be trying to solve a problem. We need to give ourselves a mental break from feeling guilty about something we said or did yesterday. Face it. We will never solve all the world's problems or handle every situation exactly as we should. We can let go of those thoughts. Those are not the ones we're told to linger on.

This doesn't mean that we should be naïve or ignore problems, hoping they sort themselves out. We live in the world. We're going to face some unlovely things that require our attention. However, God's peace follows obedience. We're told to think and dwell on the good and praiseworthy things. When we do that, we find God's peace. This is one way your Creator takes care of you and guards your mind.

Friends, it is not a trivial thing to think good thoughts. It's a direct line to God.

Action: It is more than OK to think good thoughts. Right now, in this moment, meditate on something lovely and praiseworthy. Make time for this every day.

HE GIVES AGAIN

AND HE SAID: "NAKED I CAME FROM MY MOTHER'S WOMB,
AND NAKED SHALL I RETURN THERE. THE LORD GAVE,
AND THE LORD HAS TAKEN AWAY; BLESSED BE THE NAME
OF THE LORD."

—JOB 1:21

Did you know that the phrase "the Lord gives, and the Lord takes away" comes from the Old Testament book of Job? Many of us can vouch for how true it is. One day as I was walking, my mind drifted to some things that I perceive as losses. On the scorecard of my life, they remain losses. Nothing changes that fact.

As my mind began to tally those losses, that phrase hit me square—"The Lord gives, and the Lord takes away." I didn't know the exact verse it was, but I knew it was found in Job. You probably know the short version of the story. Job was quite wealthy and very blessed. He had land, livestock, servants, and the perfect number and ratio of children (four boys and three girls). Job was upright in the eyes of God and was blessed.

God allowed Satan to wreak havoc in Job's life, and he lost everything. Job's immediate response was that phrase from verse 21. He still blessed the name of the Lord even after his livestock, servants, and children were gone.

That is where God pressed on my heart. I thought about how God gives and takes away, and in my spirit, I felt Him saying, "But I give again." Chills and understanding washed all over me. My brain raced, thinking about Job and about the losses in my life. I realized if I only focused on my losses, I was missing the big picture.

In my experience (Job's too), the Lord gives again. After losing his health and receiving some poor counsel from his friends, Job stayed faithful to the Lord. As a result, God intervened and ultimately restored Job's losses (42:10). He was given twice as much as he had before. The word *restore* is key here. God didn't replace; He restored. He didn't suddenly make Job a king or give him a different life or a different purpose. He restored his losses. He gave him more livestock and more children and blessed the latter half of his life more than the first.

It hit me then how I am sad specifically about relationships that I've lost—some to death, others to, well, life—but then on just how much God has restored. I have other relationships that have filled those empty places. I have more because of the losses. How blessed we are that when we remain faithful to Him, God can restore our losses, and He is glorified through our experience. Because He is the only one who can restore, our faith is strengthened.

How much would it bless you and bless others who see you to look beyond the loss and toward what God gives again? I'm thankful today that "the Lord takes away" doesn't need to be end of the story. Restoration is real.

Action: Remember your losses, and then, if you're staying faithful, look to see where and how God is doing a restoration in your life. If He hasn't done it yet, get ready.

Summer

LESSON FROM THE TREES

BUT LET EACH ONE EXAMINE HIS OWN WORK, AND THEN
HE WILL HAVE REJOICING IN HIMSELF ALONE, AND NOT
IN ANOTHER. FOR EACH ONE SHALL BEAR HIS OWN LOAD.

—GALATIANS 6:4–5

I often run the last stretch of my daily walk. This extra effort ensures that when I finish, I am pouring sweat and breathing harder than normal. I walk around in my driveway to catch my breath. One late summer day as I was doing this, I looked up and noticed two trees in my yard that are just a few feet apart on the same side of my house. In theory, their conditions are basically the same.

That day, one tree was still as gloriously full and green as it had been in June. On the other one, you could count the remaining leaves. That tree is always the first to bloom and the first to lose its leaves.

I understand they are different types of trees. This is normal and expected. Year in and year out, the differences in those trees remind me of the dangers of comparing ourselves with other people.

God made us similar but different. We are not supposed to be on the exact same schedule as everyone else. That is normal and acceptable. We don't all get through life with the same skill sets, desires, gifts, bag of tools, or pace. That's OK because we're not required to run anyone else's race.

We grow and learn at different rates. What a boring world it would be if we were all the same and did everything at the same pace. Life is not a sprint to see who can do and accumulate the most. I have friends who have skills and strengths I don't have. However, I have gifts they do not have.

Truthfully, we don't know God's purpose for everyone else. We are to obey Him and take care of ourselves. He made us exactly how He wanted us. Spending time focused on why we are different from someone else or why we appear to lack their skills is unproductive. It also reflects disrespect to God and us. We each have our own unique strengths and gifts. We're expected to use them accordingly.

Each spring, that one tree blooms before all the others. It brings me hope, proclaiming warmer, sunnier days are on the way. It's full of blooms before the buds are out on the other one. One is good for my boys to climb. The other is good for providing shade. Those trees are just feet apart, but they're so different, and both are needed for what they provide.

Friends, you and the gifts you provide are desperately needed. Just as you are. Let's stop getting distracted by comparison and focus on being the best version of ourselves. Let's rest when it's time and thrive when it's time. We all have value and purpose. We're all needed.

Action: Make a list of some strengths and skills God gave you. Reflect on how you have already used them and can continue to use them for His glory.

Are We Starting to Stink?

And the satraps, administrators, governors, and the king's counselors gathered together, and they saw these men on whose bodies the fire had no power; the hair of their head was not singed nor were their garments affected, and the smell of fire was not on them.

—Daniel 3:27

Wednesday is garbage pickup day in my neighborhood. Since my husband or sons take it out to the curb 98 percent of the time, I seldom think about it. That is until those summer mornings when I happen to walk before the garbage truck has been driven through. When I pass one of those containers, the air is pungent.

This is not a problem in the winter. Heat makes the stench worse as warmer temperatures help turn liquids and solids into gases, which in turn have more odor. In short, it's more stinky. The same holds true for people when heat is applied. Physically, we get sweaty and start to stink.

What about the rest of life when problems make us feel like the heat has turned up? Do we let that heat work on us and then choose poorly? What if we chase people away from God because the heat got to us, and our choices made us stink?

In the story of the fiery furnace (in the book of Daniel), Shadrach, Meshach, and Abednego held up under the fire of King Nebuchadnezzar, who wanted them to worship him. They refused, the fire was turned up, and they were thrown in. God protected them in the fire so much that "the smell of the fire was not on them." The king even came away praising God because their convictions didn't melt when the heat was on.

Daniel had a similar experience. He felt the heat of the king's orders and that of being thrown into a lion's den. His convictions held up, and God held onto him. Again, the king praised God. God was glorified because those men did not melt in the heat. They trusted God in their hearts, and their actions proved it.

We have make-or-break moments throughout life that God uses for His infinite glory. When the heat gets turned up on us, we must decide how to react. Choose to trust God or not. We each get opportunities to put into practice the faith we talk about.

There are times when right and wrong may seem unclear, and suddenly life feels hot. We have a choice in those times, and we most often have to make it through the heat. Choose God and His way or choose the fire. Choose Him.

As the heat gets turned up, I pray for more faith for all of us who could be on the verge of starting to stink. I pray that like Shadrach, Meshach, Abednego, and Daniel, we can live out our convictions and practice what we preach. I pray that we can be found being relentlessly obedient to God, praising Him when it's unpopular, and trusting Him to protect us from the heat.

Let us replace the stench of hot garbage with the sweet aroma of praise.

Action: Regardless of your situation, spend time praising God. Think of it like deodorant for your life.

Maintain Your Treasures

"For where your treasure is, there your heart will be also."

—Matthew 6:21

One of my friends has a neighbor who put new potted plants outside her front door three different times one summer, only to let them die. My friend had one potted plant outside her door that grew full and lush. She watered and talked to her plant, while the neighbor failed to care for her plants.

My summer routine is to water and deadhead my outdoor plants each day when I finish my walk. Picking off the dead blooms encourages more growth and keeps the plants looking better. On my walks, I see neighbors working on their landscapes—mowing, edging, pulling weeds, watering.

We put up a small pool for the kids. It was good investment, but it took work. It was too big to change the water with every usage but too small to have all the equipment that regulates the chemicals. I shocked it. I added chlorine. I tested the pH. I cleaned the filter. I scooped out grass, leaves, and random bugs. I spent time on it almost every day.

Plants and pools are great examples of the importance of maintenance. Almost everything worth having requires maintenance and upkeep to ensure that it lasts and fully serves its purpose. If we want to keep our teeth, we need to brush them and have regular dental checkups. We eat vegetables and exercise to maintain our physical health.

Relationships require regular maintenance as well. Strong, dependable relationships need to be watered and weeded to grow and bloom. Whether it's marriage, friendship, or our relationship with Christ, it takes regular work and care.

Conceptually, this is easy to understand. Maybe it's harder than I think because I spend a lot of time emphasizing it to my children. We must take care of our treasures if we want them to last and perform optimally.

It seems this is harder with some things than others. The motivation behind it is really the difference. I bet my friend's neighbor knows she needs to water plants, but it isn't a high priority to her. I want my kids to be able to play in their pool, so keeping it usable is essential.

The Bible says our hearts are aligned with our treasures, and as such, we maintain them. What are you treasuring? What parts of your life need maintenance? Do you want those parts to last, or are they like weeds and dead flowers on a plant—just choking out the good stuff?

If we want our lives and our relationships to thrive, we must consistently do the work of maintenance. We must care for what we want to grow. That may require us to trim off what is dead, or maybe we need to add something. This requires paying attention and being prepared to work.

The Bible tells us earthly treasures decay and are easily stolen. They don't last. If the maintenance of the temporary takes away too much time from the lasting, maybe it's time to rethink what we're treasuring. Where's your heart, friends? Do you need to do some maintenance in your life? Now's a good time.

Action: Take stock of what you treasure. Perform necessary maintenance.

No Vacation from Gratitude

I CONSIDER THAT OUR PRESENT SUFFERINGS ARE NOT
WORTH COMPARING WITH THE GLORY THAT WILL BE
REVEALED IN US.

—ROMANS 8:18

My husband, children, and I had just returned from a much-needed vacation. Sadly, death had gotten in the way, and we hadn't taken one in two years. Trust me when I say it was needed.

It was a different one for me, as it was the first time in my adult life I wasn't vacationing from a paying job. Until my oldest started kindergarten, I worked outside the home. Since then, I've been working from home. The ability to work wherever I want is a perk. My work is evolving. I closed my business and am trusting God on a new writing path. This involves me putting in a lot of work time that no one sees, and I may or may not ever make money from it.

I mention that only to emphasize I'm functioning in a different type of working environment. I wasn't taking a break from an employer. I only took a vacation from my house, cooking, exercise, and arguably my better judgment. I did not need to have ice cream four times while we were gone, but I did. What's done is done, and that is what a vacation is for after all!

Taking a vacation from my good sense comes with a price. I would make those same decisions again, providing it's only once or twice a year. My bank account and scales both verify the cost of my vacation.

After making it safely home, I went for my morning walk the next day to get back in my usual routine. As I walked, I was thinking about how different it was to not be taking a vacation from anything. I didn't really need rest; I just needed to be somewhere else. I needed some time to have fun with my family sans a few responsibilities. We can ditch some of those responsibilities for a few days. We can rest from labor. We can take a break from being the version of ourselves we present to the world. Those are needed breaks.

I am glad God doesn't take a vacation. I'm just grateful. I thought about it for a full week after returning home. Grateful to have uninterrupted time with my husband and children. Grateful to play with them and love on them. Grateful that we were able to safely find a way to take a vacation and grateful to have a home to come back to.

We're often focused on what we don't have, what we can't do, where we can't go, or what we don't like. I'm guilty of getting caught up in that mentality. It's not helpful. What is helpful is focusing on what we do have and being grateful.

I'm reminded of one of my favorite Bible verses, found in Romans 8:18, which says sufferings today can't compare to the coming glory. It reminds me to be grateful.

I'm grateful to serve God by writing words. I am grateful to structure a life that works for my family. I am grateful to keep my life-giving routines in place. I am grateful for the loving, saving, and keeping grace of Jesus and that it never takes a vacation.

Action: Make a list of things you're grateful for.

X Marks the Spot

Through the Lord's mercies we are not consumed, Because His compassions fail not. They are new every morning; Great is Your faithfulness.

—Lamentations 3:22–23

As an attempt to get them outdoors, my husband told our boys that there were Xs and other markings painted on the streets in our neighborhood. They took off on bikes like they were searching for treasure. A while later, they showed back up red-faced, sweaty, and aggravated.

"That was not very nice," they huffed. "There were no Xs out there, and what we saw has been there forever. That wasn't anything special."

I informed them that no one said it was special or new—just that there were markings painted on the streets. I later walked with them and pointed some out. These were markings and numbers that had been applied by the utility companies. They were not placed there by a spy on a secret mission.

It was interesting to me that they never paid attention to what was right in front of them all along. But aren't we all guilty of that from time to time? Downtime at home during the pandemic forced me to see what and who I truly value. I saw that it can be easy to look beyond what's right in front of us.

My kids built up an adventure in their minds, and reality just couldn't live up to it. They were disappointed. I have struggled with this often. We have all experienced disappointments. A sports season cancelled. An event postponed. A vacation not taken. Time with our important people lost.

My boys didn't appreciate what they got from their adventure—fresh air, sunshine, exercise, time together, freedom, memories. That is a long list when you think about it. I thought about some of my pandemic-related disappointments. A vacation cancelled. Finishing a school year at home. A missed sports season, trips to concerts, and ball games. Lost time with friends and family. All disappointing.

But we also found benefits. The boys camped in the yard and went on neighborhood adventures. We had movie marathons and Bible school at home. We had the most accidental, low-key, fun Fourth of the July spaced out across yards with neighbors. We saw fireworks all around and lightning bugs in the yard. Who knew that you could enjoy both at once in your lot of suburbia? We spent time making the ordinary special.

Looking back, things that were originally disappointments fueled some wonderful moments. My children will grow up and remember a lot of fantastic times from a summer full of cancellations. I pray they've learned a little about what to do when life hands you lemons. When life gives disappointments, look for God's mercies, which are new every morning. We don't have to accept those lemons and stay stuck in disappointment. It's OK to acknowledge them and to be disappointed, but it is not good to stay stuck there. We can shift our focus off the disappointments and onto the promises of God's mercies each day. Make it your own version of a treasure hunt. You won't be disappointed.

Action: Think about one of your most recent disappointments. Now find God's mercy in it.

Change When It's Time

One September morning as I walked, I noticed a single bright orange leaf on a tree that was still full of green leaves. I could see it from a distance because all his friends were still green. That orange leaf stood out from the crowd. My mind was flooded with thoughts of seasons of change. We were right on the cusp of summer fading into fall, and that leaf was a sneak peek of what was coming. Visible change was on its way.

It's OK to change even if your friends aren't ready yet. Change is normal and allows real beauty to shine. Changing leaves reminds us that nothing lasts forever. There is a season for everything. Solomon spelled it all it in Ecclesiastes 3:1–8. "To everything there is a season, A time for every purpose under heaven," he begins in verse 1. If you read the full scripture, you will see it is pure poetry, but it also indicates change.

Most of us agree that change in life is inevitable. We know that God doesn't change, but we do. Our physical bodies change. Our minds change (some more often than others). God gave us brains and choice. He created us to change. He doesn't change, but we do.

But change is also often fought tooth and nail. I don't always like it. I don't care for uncertainty, not knowing what the outcome of something is going to be or how it's going to impact my life. It can be really scary, especially if we're the first in our circle to experience a change.

Friend, I won't tell you not to be scared, but I will reiterate Paul's words in 2 Corinthians 4:16, "to not lose heart." Our physical selves are changing. We're aging and experiencing challenges that come at all stages of that. However, if we have put our trust and hope in Christ, our minds and souls are being changed every day for the better.

All change, even that which we know is necessary and better for us in the long run, can give us pause. We may not have the support we would like to have. We may not know what the outcome will be. It's hard to take steps toward change we know we need. It's harder still to find our balance when change has been forced upon us.

Change is necessary. To be the people God wants us to be, we must be a work in progress. The necessary changes have to happen at their appropriate time. We can count on seasons of change just like we can count on a God who stays the same. He is the compass, the benchmark, the anchor, the goal that we are striving to reach. To be all He made us to be.

As we move from one season to the next on the calendar and in life, may we all embrace it and gracefully change when it's our time.

Action: Ask God to show you where you need to make changes. Take one step in that direction each day.

WALKING THROUGH

YEA, THOUGH I WALK THROUGH THE VALLEY OF THE
SHADOW OF DEATH, I WILL FEAR NO EVIL; FOR YOU ARE
WITH ME; YOUR ROD AND YOUR STAFF, THEY COMFORT ME.

—PSALM 23:4

I was on my walk the day after my father-in-law's funeral when it dawned on me that his funeral was on the anniversary of the estate sale for my parents' belongings, house, and property the year before. My husband, children, and I have been put through the grief wringer in the last few years as my boys lost both grandfathers in back-to-back summers.

The number of hard days that we have faced overwhelmed my thoughts that day. I couldn't find the right words to describe my feelings until I saw a quote on a Facebook post from popular Christian singer TobyMac that said, "Just keep showing up when most people would quit." I know without a doubt how important this is from repeated personal experience. We get through the hard stuff by refusing to quit. If you haven't faced hard days yet, you had better lace up your hiking boots.

Friends, the key word is *through*. We all go through hard stuff sooner or later. The way to make it through is to keep showing up for your life and for your people. God brought to mind the words of the twenty-third psalm. Many of you probably know it by heart. It's ironic to me that this portion of scripture speaks to my grief journey because my mom clung to those same words as she suffered through a two-year battle with cancer before leaving this life and meeting Jesus face-to-face.

It's verse 4 that God put on my heart, which tells us that we walk through the valley. We don't get to bypass it, fly over it, or lay a finger aside of our nose and magically be done with it. We walk through it. When we get to the valleys, we walk through them. That means we consistently show up and face the hard days. We keep walking. We don't stay there. We keep going.

Oh, how I pray that none of us have too many valleys to journey through in life. I've had more than I would like. I'm certain you have too. They are unpleasant. But God promises to go with us each step of the way. He comforts us, and He prepares the way for us. Friends, here's the catch: we must choose to do the walking. Then we must walk on through.

One more note about walking through. It means all the way to the other side. You will come out in a different place than you entered. I do not know where your own "through" will take you or how long it will last, but it does have an exit. If you keep going, one day you will realize you have reached that exit. You won't forget the walk though. It might change you, and you may have scars, but you can go all the way through.

I know many of you are carrying heavy stuff and growing weary of walking. Please don't quit. Keep walking until you're through.

Action: Take hold of God's hand today. Face the hard stuff. Walk on through.

When It's Hard

"Enter by the narrow gate; for wide is the gate and broad is the way that leads to destruction, and there are many who go in by it. Because narrow is the gate and difficult is the way which leads to life, and there are few who find it."

—Matthew 7:13–14

I usually try to finish my walk with about a half-mile run to finish stronger than I started. It's a personal quirk, I guess. It might seem silly because I'm not running marathons. You don't have to be facing a 26.2-mile run to develop that kind of mentality.

Truth be told, I hate running. On days when it's hot, humid, and it feels like slogging through a bowl of soup, running is even more difficult. I tried to talk myself out of walking at all on the day that God put this verse on my heart. The humidity was oppressive. It was hard to catch your breath. No one was making me do it, and anyone would understand if I didn't.

No friends, teammates, or coaches were there to push me. There have been many days in my life when I would've easily taken a pass and waited until conditions were better. I've learned many things as I've gotten older, but among those is that sometimes we must do the hard thing even when the world would give us permission to quit. It is not the world that I'm trying to please. It's my own race to run.

Sometimes the only way to get where we really want to go is to do what we don't have to do. The easy road does not take us everywhere we need to go. My walking time is valuable to me for many reasons. There are many days when I would prefer to walk and chat with a friend. Unfortunately, I've scared them away with my intensity, and none of them will walk with me. If I waited on a friend to join me, I'd never go.

If I waited for perfect conditions or for my body to feel great, I'd never go. If I waited for the easier day when I didn't have anything else to do, I'd take about two walks a year on sunny, summer Sunday evenings. I would forfeit a whole lot of benefit, enjoyment, and accomplishment if I waited for easier days and better circumstances.

The same is true in our daily walk with God. If we're unwilling to be uncomfortable sometimes or to make sacrifices, we're going to miss out on becoming who He wants us to be. Jesus said the way is narrow (Matthew 7:13–14).

Friends, don't give up because it's hard. Don't wait on ideal circumstances or on someone else. Do it now. Do it by yourself. Do it on shaking legs, with a cracking voice, with a broken heart, and with or without an audience. Do it for you. You can do it.

Action: Are you avoiding something you need to do because it will be difficult and the world says it's OK if you don't? Dig deep, ignore the world, and do the hard thing.

Count Your Blessings

GIVING THANKS ALWAYS FOR ALL THINGS TO GOD THE
FATHER IN THE NAME OF OUR LORD JESUS CHRIST.

—EPHESIANS 5:20

Do you ever just become overwhelmed with a sense of gratitude? I do. I had one of those moments one afternoon during the summer of COVID. My kids had unceremoniously finished their respective school years at home. My husband was working from home. Like many of us, we were largely confined to home in distanced learning.

I had been out for my usual walk and taken care of chores and various tasks that needed to be completed. Early in the afternoon, I went outside to sit on my deck and work on a daily Bible study I had been participating in. The kids chose that time to come outside and play in their small pool just a few feet away from me.

Often, my reaction is to get frustrated when they choose to play loudly nearby while I'm working or having some sort of quiet time. This day as I sat there in the sunshine—Bible and notebook in my lap—watching my healthy kids play happily, I was overwhelmed with gratitude. And I do mean overwhelmed. I couldn't help but think about how hard it was to function in the world as it was just then—so full of fear and uncertainty everywhere. But in that moment, I was just so thankful for so many things that it brought tears to my eyes.

My days are a gazillion times better when my focus is on counting my blessings. I'm reminded of that hymn "Count Your Blessings." The lyrics say to name them one by one and see what God has done. That's what I did that day. I thanked God for every blessing I could think of one by one. And I've been trying to do that more often since that day.

I'm not always as good at it as I would like to be, but I'm getting better. I've been really trying to make it a regular part of my day—especially on frustrating days. It is hard to stay frustrated when you literally start naming and counting your blessings.

Can I just encourage you to pause and count yours as well? It's a game changer, my friends. Psalm 105:1 says, "Oh give thanks to the Lord! Call upon His name; Make known His deeds among the peoples."

Two parts of that verse jump out to me. The first is the exclamation point. In a world of texting and social media, perhaps the exclamation has lost its weight and we overlook it. That mark shows strong emphasis on giving thanks to the Lord. Secondly, we are to "make known His deeds." Write them down. Say them out loud. Sing them. Whatever you choose, make those blessings known.

Counting your blessings requires action. When you make your gratitude known, it provides a better perspective for you, serves as an example to others, and helps glorify God. In my experience, that leads to feelings of being overwhelmed with gratitude. It lightens heavy loads and soothes weary souls. Count your blessings, friends. See what God has done.

Action: Count those blessings. Name them one by one. You'll have more than you think.

CHASING THE GOOD

I was on my morning walk and saw a fellow walker in the distance. We walk about the same time most mornings. We always speak, and sometimes I walk a few steps with him. This has played out so much that I know his routes.

This day, I was about a half a mile away when I first spotted him walking down a street perpendicular to the road I was on. I decided to see if I could catch him before he made his turn and started walking back toward me. I've chased him down like that before, but this time I was farther away.

I didn't catch him, but I got close enough that I could have hit him with a paper wad. In fact, when he made his turn and saw me, he jumped and said, "Where did you come from?" I laughed and told him again that I like trying to catch him when I'm at a good distance because it makes me push myself. I slowed down, walked a few paces with him, and chatted for a minute before I moved on at my regular speed.

I thought about the significance of that as I walked on. Sometimes it's important to have that pace car ahead of you. It didn't hurt me to push myself harder. It made my exercise more effective. It helps to show us what we're capable of when we push ourselves. But I wasn't in a race. My thoughts began to shift from the physical to the spiritual.

I began to think about how important it is to have people who serve as examples in life. Mentors and others help show us what to expect and what's possible. They give us direction, confidence, and a goal to chase.

We need to be careful of who we're looking up to as an example, but I believe God sends each of us some good ones. The apostle Paul talked about being good examples for Christ. Scripture tells us to be imitators of Christ, to follow His example, and to meditate on good and noble things.

There are people out there handling bad days well, doing good instead of evil, and living as God wants them to. They are wonderful examples to follow. They serve as encouragement to us. They help give us direction and light the path we're walking. We may never catch them, but we can try. Those people help make us better people.

Look for these people in your life. They can help you find your spark—even if they don't know it. They're out there, some closer than others. Use their good example of imitating Christ to see that it's possible and that it makes a difference. You may not realize it, but someone is probably looking to you for the same thing. Let's try to chase down good examples, and let's set a better pace for those who are looking at us.

Action: Ask God to point out worthy mentors in your life who can help you reach your potential.

FOUNDATION ON THE ROCK

A new housing development is taking shape adjacent to my neighborhood. Some homes are occupied, and others are in various stages of being built. I've been watching the progress of one of these houses during my walks.

I have watched the framing go up day by day. Then the walls, the roof, and the windows. My daily walk has also given me a look at home improvements happening in my neighborhood. Getting the foundation right is the key to anything we build.

As I have watched those homes being built and improvements being made, I realized that lately I've been making my own improvements in my gratitude. Coming out of a season of grief has made me dig deeper to find exactly what I am thankful for. Rest assured, I am thankful, and each time I think about what it is I am grateful for, the answer is the same. It is my foundation. I am grateful for my parents and the time I had with them, but even more so, I am grateful that they took me to church and taught me about Jesus.

Nothing on earth is meant to last, including people we love, no matter how much we love them. Earthly foundations will eventually fall, but I was given a foundation that will stand and not crumble when faced with the heaviest of storms. Our foundations will be tested; of that I am 100 percent convinced. Having my foundation built on the rock of Jesus is what I am absolutely the most grateful for. It is the only thing that holds no matter the strength of life's storms.

The time to make sure our foundation or the foundation we are building for our children is sound is right now. Cosmetic improvements are fine for sunny days, but they don't hold up in stormy weather. Even the sun will fade them in time. Invest in your foundation and the foundation of the people you love. This is what is of eternal value.

Isaiah 54:11 says, "O you afflicted one, tossed with tempest, and not comforted, Behold, I will lay your stones with colorful gems, And lay your foundations with sapphires." I love this verse and so much of this chapter. When we are in the worst of storms, God's foundation is precious and valuable. He promises peace, protection, and freedom from fear. These are benefits of having the right foundation.

We don't have to fear the storms when our foundation is built on Christ. They won't prevail against us. We can make it through our most challenging storms. A foundation built on the rock is worth the investment.

Action: How's your foundation? If it needs repairs, fix it now before the next storm comes.

JACKHAMMERING

So he answered and said, "'You shall love the Lord your God with all your heart, with all your soul, with all your strength, and with all your mind,' and 'your neighbor as yourself.'"

—Luke 10:27

I had a few extra minutes one morning and was watching the rain through my front window. My eyes were drawn to my newly repaved street, which led my thoughts back to my walks on the previous couple days. I had noticed workers jackhammering parts of what was now freshly paved while they had been fixing access points to the water and sewer lines.

It struck me then how we often do something similar with our hearts. We pave over them in hopes that the going will be smooth. We cover up our damaged places. But when we do that, we block access to places we need—places that house love and vulnerability.

These are vital resources to long-term stability. That smooth paving job might seem wonderful to everyone else, but it's imperative to our relationships, especially our relationship with God, that we remember to keep these access points open.

We have all made mistakes, handled situations incorrectly, and done things we're not proud of. Things we don't want to share with the world. We try to cover them up, ignore them, and hope they don't get out. That might work for our fringe relationships or on social media, but it doesn't cut it with our closest people. And it certainly doesn't cut it with God.

God wants access to our whole heart. We can't just offer Him the parts we deem acceptable and then cover up the rest because we're ashamed, feel guilty, or don't trust Him. Jeremiah 17:9 says, "The heart is deceitful above all things, and desperately wicked; Who can know it?" God knows how messed up our hearts can be, but He loves us and wants them anyway.

Once we give Him access to our entire heart, healing can begin. In Psalm 51:10, David sets an example for us. "Create in me a clean heart, O God, And renew a steadfast spirit within me." In Ezekiel 36:26, God says, "I will give you a new heart and put a new spirit within you; I will take the heart of stone out of your flesh and give you a heart of flesh."

Friends, we're not fooling God by trying to cover up pieces of our hearts in the hopes that we can ignore them. He wants us to trust Him with our vulnerable places. Only He can truly fix our hearts. He purifies and renews. It's opening up, not covering up, that repairs hearts. But He won't do it without our invitation.

We must let Him in to experience the renewal and the eternal life He promises. It's up to you to decide. Do you have any places that need some jackhammering today? Don't be afraid to make some safe access points and let Him in.

Action: What are you trying to hide from God? Let Him in and give your heart to Him.

SHADOWS

FOR THE LAW, HAVING A SHADOW OF THE GOOD THINGS
TO COME, AND NOT THE VERY IMAGE OF THE THINGS,
CAN NEVER WITH THESE SAME SACRIFICES, WHICH THEY
OFFER CONTINUALLY YEAR BY YEAR, MAKE THOSE WHO
APPROACH PERFECT.

—HEBREWS 10:1

One bright, sunshiny morning, I was walking and noticed my shadow in front of me. I was going uphill, and it was all I could pay attention to. I don't know why it caught my attention, but it was so drastic I kept thinking about it.

To have a shadow means there is a source of light. In this case, it was the sun. *Merriam-Webster* defines a shadow as "the dark figure cast upon a surface by a body intercepting the rays from a source of light." I love the idea that I was intercepting rays of sunshine. But it's the shadow that got me.

It resembled me in a funhouse mirror. I watched my arms swing, my quarantine ponytail bouncing back and forth, and my shape shift with every step. I had a shrunken head, long arms, and then a foot the size of a boat. It was 100 percent me except that it wasn't. It was only an imitation of me.

James 1:17 says good things come from the Father, and there's no shadow of turning. The part that struck me about this is it is a reminder that God is the light. He is reliable, dependable, and doesn't change. My shadow was changing with every movement, and I caused the shape shifting.

I become frustrated with a world that is constantly shifting. God doesn't change. There is no variation. When we focus more on Him and less on the shadows cast by people, our world settles.

Then I thought about the phrase used in multiple Bible verses, "a shadow of good things to come." Hebrews 10:1 talks about sacrifices having been a shadow of good things to come. Clearly Jesus—the ultimate sacrifice. My shadow was a poor substitute for the real me that was just behind it.

I wonder how many times I've given up at the "shadow of good things" and didn't stick around for the actual good things. I am guilty of accepting good enough. That is too bad because the good God has for us is far better than good enough. It's like my kids settling for a popsicle when they could have had an ice-cream cone.

God doesn't change. He is reliable. He delivers on His promises for hope and a good future. It won't be shadows but the real deal. If we settle, we've got ourselves to blame.

How do we know when it's the real deal from God or just a shadow of something coming? We must want to know. We must pray and let Him answer. He will not let you mess up the timing. God can get your attention. Don't get lost in the shadows and miss the light. Friends, if you're stuck focusing on the shadows, turn around.

Action: Turn toward the light.

Fall

RAINBOWS

Real talk today, friends. I went out for my walk one morning, not realizing that it was going to rain. It did, and I got soaking wet. It never poured, but it never stopped. My clothes, socks, shoes—everything was soaking wet, enough that my clothes got heavier, and my toes wrinkled from the moisture. I thought about cutting it short and heading back, but it didn't matter once I was already soaked, so I kept on.

And I'm glad I did. If I had known it was going to rain that substantially, I likely wouldn't have gone out. I would have cheated myself out of needed exercise and out of seeing a rainbow suddenly appear and then gently disappear. In that moment, it felt like God saying, "It's going to be OK."

What a gift it was that morning to walk in the rain. Seeing that rainbow and remembering God's promise to Noah and all future generations that He would not flood the earth again came to mind. But it wasn't just about not flooding that stirred my soul that day.

It was on a day deep into a pandemic summer full of COVID-19 and all the various challenges and debates that came with it. It sure had been feeling to me like a cloud was hanging over the world. The rainbow and that deep feeling in my bones from the Lord that it would be OK was a reminder that God loves us and keeps His promises.

That day, I could have sunk into anger, self-pity, sadness, maybe even fear. It would have been understandable and justifiable if I had. Friend, it's understandable and justifiable for any of us when we're caught in the middle of the rain and clouds of life. It would have made perfect sense for me not to walk that day. You could argue that it would have been smarter to not go. Oh, but what I would have missed.

When my eyes and thoughts shifted to the rainbow and God's promises, the rain no longer mattered. In light of God's promise, the clouds and the rain were just temporary. I felt that promise, like a hug from God, through my whole being. That promise is not just for me. It's for you too.

God is still right with you on the rainy, cloudy days. He doesn't disappear or leave you to fend for yourself. He can make your hard days worthwhile. He is dependable and keeps His word to never leave you or forsake you. He is faithful.

Don't let a rainy day or cloudy season keep you from holding tight to the promises of God.

Action: Don't let the rain stop you. Use it as time to dwell on God's promises.

CRACKS IN THE ARMOR

"A GOOD MAN OUT OF THE GOOD TREASURE OF HIS HEART
BRINGS FORTH GOOD THINGS, AND AN EVIL MAN OUT OF
THE EVIL TREASURE BRINGS FORTH EVIL THINGS."

—MATTHEW 12:35

Confession time. I don't like to admit it, but sometimes there are cracks in my armor. I've been through my share of life's battles, and normally, I hold up well enough. What I've discovered, though, is that just when you've managed to survive some big stuff, little things will gang up on you and point out the cracks in your armor.

For me, these cracks usually show when I've been yelling at kids or have been short with my husband or my friends for reasons they may have nothing to do with. I'm not proud of myself in those moments. After one particularly rough week, I was thinking about those cracks as I walked.

God planted another thought on that walk as I passed by a wooden privacy fence that I've walked by many times in all sorts of weather. That day, I was absolutely struck by the sunshine streaming through the cracks in that fence. There were sunny patches that streaked the otherwise frost-covered grass. The grass needed that light from the sun. This absolutely blew me away in that moment.

Certainly, there is something to be said for the protection offered by a fence or armor or a hardened heart and closed-off emotions. But God used that fence to show me that there is something to be said for the cracks too. Light gets through them. Friend, I could cry right now letting this wash over me again.

God reminded me of Matthew 12:35, which says, "A good man out of the good treasure of his heart brings forth good things, and an evil man out of the evil treasure brings forth evil things." Similarly, my mom always told me, "What goes in is what comes out." If cracks are beginning to show in our armor, whatever shines out is a reflection of what we have been putting in.

When we eat too much, we gain weight. That's an easy example. When we don't like what's coming through, we need to examine what's going in. As Proverbs 4:23 says, "Keep your heart with all diligence, for out of it spring the issues of life."

When I notice those cracks, it might be that I took my eyes off Jesus. Maybe I have chosen to dwell on my mistakes instead of giving myself enough grace to have feelings and weaknesses. Cracks in our armor are normal, but we want to be sure that it is light coming through those cracks. The way to do that is to put good things in.

Consuming better might look like watching less news and spending more time in prayer. It might look like spending less time on social media and more time interacting with our children. Whatever it looks like for you, I pray it includes giving yourself enough grace to allow for some cracks. I pray that lots of light streams through to the people in your path.

Action: Think of one change, either in adding or giving up, that you can make this week in what you're consuming. Now give it a try.

FAITH THROUGH FOG

NOW FAITH IS THE SUBSTANCE OF THINGS HOPED FOR, THE
EVIDENCE OF THINGS NOT SEEN.

—HEBREWS 11:1

Walking on autumn mornings often means walking through fog. It is ironic that I see so much when the conditions for sight aren't favorable. I think the fog makes me pay more attention. Plus, it literally gets stuck on my eyelashes, so I can't miss it.

One such morning, I left my driveway and could only see a small distance. Because I knew what was ahead, I knew the road would veer hard to the right. If I hadn't known where I was and couldn't see ahead, I might have become skeptical of continuing.

There are times when fog comes into our life, and our visibility feels low. Change happens, and it leaves us with an unclear path ahead. This is when life requires faith and obedience. I'm in a foggy patch of life right now. I'm 100 percent sure God wants me to write, but I don't know what exactly. The path ahead is foggy.

Here's what I do know. God is only asking me to take one step at a time. He doesn't ask me to make the turn before I get there. He just asks me to trust Him on the direction.

Slow down, friends. Faith requires us to take one step at a time even when we can't see where the road is going. Hebrews 11:1 says, "Now faith is the substance of things hoped for, the evidence of things not seen."

There is so much truth about faith to be found in Hebrews chapter 11. Go hang out there for a while and read those words of truth. You'll be glad you did. If you read up to verse 6, notice that without faith, it is impossible to please God.

Impossible—that's pretty absolute! If we want to please God, we must exercise our faith. We must become comfortable with the fog. We need to keep taking one step at a time, and the way will clear. I can't see the whole street, but when I get to a turn, I can see it. It keeps opening just in front of me. One step at a time, I can see the road ahead as I keep stepping into faith.

Sometimes that looks like saying yes. Sometimes it looks like an unpopular choice or having a different opinion. It's risky. It feels scary. Often, no one else understands, or they think you're crazy.

We want to know everything up front. Knowing what's up ahead gives us the illusion that we're in control. That we've got things figured out. That we're prepared. That we don't have to change. That we can figure out the way to go or how to do things and settle in for the long haul. But life comes with fog.

Friend, take your steps of faith into the unknown. It's OK to walk into the fog. Get so close that your eyelashes get wet. This kind of faith is more valuable than gold, according to 1 Peter. You will please God, and He will show you the way as you go.

Action: What is one step in the direction of faith for you today? Take it.

FLAWED BUT BLOOMING

NOT THAT I HAVE ALREADY ATTAINED, OR AM ALREADY
PERFECTED; BUT I PRESS ON, SO THAT I MAY LAY HOLD
OF THAT WHICH CHRIST JESUS HAS ALSO LAID HOLD
OF ME. BRETHREN, I DO NOT COUNT MYSELF TO HAVE
APPREHENDED; BUT ONE THING I DO, FORGETTING THOSE
THINGS WHICH ARE BEHIND AND REACHING FORWARD TO
THOSE THINGS WHICH ARE AHEAD, I PRESS ON TOWARD
THE GOAL FOR THE PRIZE OF THE UPWARD CALL OF GOD
IN JESUS CHRIST.

—PHILIPPIANS 3:12–14

I s there such a thing as a spirit flower? I hear people referring to spirit animals, but since I'm not an animal person, I think I should have a spirit flower. So, I've decided mine is a morning glory.

Morning glories get their name because they are at their best in early morning. They are a low-maintenance vining flower that thrives on the support of fences, arches, and such. Get this … their blooms are shaped like a trumpet, almost as if they have something to say.

There are much cooler plants, like the sunflower or the lotus, but I connect with the morning glory. I'm at my best in the morning. I'll grow on you over time. I'm incredibly low maintenance, and while I may choose to be quiet, I almost always have something to trumpet.

There's a morning glory growing on a fence that I walk by. One fall day, I noticed that I could just see a handful of blooms left. I got up close and took a picture. And that was when I really felt connected with this specific flower. It was hanging out there by itself. It was wrinkled, weathered, and scarred all around but was still blooming anyway, while its friends had given up and withered away. It was still blooming, flaws and all. I desperately wanted to be like that.

It made me think of pressing on regardless of our inadequacies. Despite its imperfections, that flower was still trumpeting beauty and hope. Can we be vulnerable enough to provide that kind of hope for one another?

When life takes its toll, we become weathered and scarred. We try to present our best, unaffected selves to the world, and we might not even notice one another's flaws from a distance. I think I tend to do this to convince myself I'm fine and the world hasn't gotten the best of me. But if you get up close, you're going to see my flaws. We can't hide them. And we shouldn't. They make us who we are. God uses them, and we grow. I don't know anyone who hasn't been scarred up by life. If it looks like someone hasn't been, you're not close enough. What you see is the beauty of someone pressing on despite the brokenness.

We've all made damaging mistakes. Ask for forgiveness, leave mistakes behind, and press on. If we get too caught up in what's behind, we lose sight of what's ahead. Not everything can be fixed. The mistake is getting so caught up in perceived brokenness that we can't move on.

Don't get stuck on your flaws, mistakes, and scars. Give them to God and let Him make them beautiful. Press on. Bloom anyway.

Action: Think of a mistake or flaw you are currently struggling with. Ask God for forgiveness and to help you let it go. Allow yourself to bloom.

THE GIFT OF ORDINARY

LET YOUR CONDUCT BE WITHOUT COVETOUSNESS, AND
BE CONTENT WITH SUCH THINGS AS YOU HAVE. FOR
HE HIMSELF HAS SAID, "I WILL NEVER LEAVE YOU NOR
FORSAKE YOU."

—HEBREWS 13:5

One morning as I walked, I was overwhelmed with an ordinary view. I saw a gray sky devoid of distinguishing features. Just a vastness of gray. I saw the same path that I walk every day, which was then lined with barren trees. The grass had browned.

I thought about how I was going to finish my same walk, by the same houses, in the same basic amount of time and go back into my very ordinary brick house. Then I would wash the same clothes I've washed many times before and pick up the same messes that I pick up daily. I was on the verge of being consumed with that feeling of ordinary when God reminded me of the busyness of previous days and lessons I am learning.

In the previous nine school days, I had been at my children's schools five times for different activities. There were club meetings, practices, birthday parties, and a lunch with a friend. I went on a school field trip and came home thinking I'd had too much day and not enough coffee. It was an unusually busy stretch of days. It was overstimulating. Perhaps the ordinariness I experienced on that walk was more noticeable because of those busy days. Was God showing me I had been too busy? Maybe.

But maybe it was something more. I felt as if God was pushing me toward gratitude … not for the busy but for the ordinary.

We should be thankful for ordinary. Ordinary is a gift. My mind flipped through conversations from the busy stretch, and I saw how each of us is working our way through struggles. Several people had asked me to pray for difficult situations. I think those people would love some ordinary days.

We often don't notice ordinary until it's gone. When it's been stripped from us, we crave it. I had been dreading that approaching Christmas following my dad's death because it was going to scream that ordinary was gone. Death forces us to find a new ordinary, and we miss our old ordinary.

God uses ordinary people, ordinary stuff, and ordinary circumstances every day. The Bible is full of examples of how God is in the ordinary. As we read in Hebrews 13:5, He will not leave us. This reminds me that my ordinary life is enough because God is in it. I don't need to chase busyness. I don't need extraordinary skills. I don't need more. I should be content with ordinary.

God elevates ordinary. God turns the water into wine. God heals the sick. God comforts us beyond comprehension when He has said no to earthly healing. God turns our pain and suffering into something good. Into hope. Into the miraculous. God gives the gift of ordinary without the pressure and exhaustion of extra.

I'm thankful for my ordinary existence; for my common life. I'm thankful for gray skies that help me appreciate the blue ones, for all of nature's seasons, for a body that can walk, and for laundry that represents people I love. I'm thankful for a God who became ordinary for us.

Action: Appreciate your ordinary life.

FEW THINGS ARE NEEDED

DO NOT BE ANXIOUS ABOUT ANYTHING, BUT IN EVERYTHING
BY PRAYER AND SUPPLICATION WITH THANKSGIVING LET
YOUR REQUESTS BE MADE KNOWN TO GOD; AND THE PEACE
OF GOD, WHICH SURPASSES ALL UNDERSTANDING, WILL
GUARD YOUR HEARTS AND MINDS THROUGH CHRIST JESUS.

—PHILIPPIANS 4:6–7

I walked out into a sketchy-looking morning heavy with fog. As I finished mile one, I could see the fog lifting in the distance. It was interesting to watch. You really can't see it happening; you just notice that it has. My thoughts spilled into the similarities of reengaging into life during the pandemic.

My kids were back in their brick-and-mortar school. I had reservations, but for our family, the reasons to go outweighed keeping them at home. It felt like fog lifting. I couldn't see it but noticed it had lifted more and more with each nugget of normal.

We resumed soccer, fall baseball, and other activities that fill up our calendar. I felt like we had been shot out of a cannon then. I heard the word *overwhelmed* from multiple friends, so it wasn't just me.

This was to be expected, given how long we had been flying low by minimizing activities and contacts. Overwhelm can cause problems quickly. I am not sure I want to go back again to that pace of feeling like I'm chasing something or running to and from activities, and then nothing matters except ticking the boxes. I don't want to live life out of control.

It makes my soul weary. I don't make good decisions. I sacrifice people and priorities I don't really want to sacrifice. I become a version of me I don't like, and it happens just like the fog lifts. Luke 10, when Jesus visits the home of Martha and her sister Mary, is a good example of this. Mary calmly sat and listened to Jesus. Martha, on the other hand, did what many of us would do with pop-in company: she worked.

She was frustrated with Mary and complained to Jesus. Verses 41 and 42 are the real gold of this passage. "Martha, Martha," the Lord answered, "you are worried and upset about many things, but few things are needed—or indeed only one. Mary has chosen what is better, and it will not be taken away from her."

Few things are needed. Let's not lose sight of that as the fog begins to lift. Do you remember how it felt when we first were stuck at home and everything was cancelled? Many people talked about appreciating bonus time with family. Others developed a better understanding of who and what their real priorities were. We took notice of people we missed and people we cared enough to check on.

We don't have to be full throttle with so many preparations and activities that we forget what's important. Let's be cautious with what and how much we go back to. Let's be more like Mary and keep our attention not on all the things that could be done but rather on the things that matter.

Philippians 4:6–7 reminds us that peace comes from God. Like the fog, we won't notice it happening, just that it has.

Action: Ask God for help in aligning your priorities.

SHARE YOUR STORY

COME AND HEAR, ALL OF YOU WHO FEAR GOD, AND I WILL
DECLARE WHAT HE HAS DONE FOR MY SOUL.

—PSALM 66:16

I love watching the leaves change color in the fall. They can be stunningly gorgeous. There is one tree I pass on my morning walks that had me fascinated for several days. It looked like it was changing from the inside out. Most of the vibrant color was closer to the trunk, and it was still more green on the farthest limbs.

I posted a picture of it on my social media because it was pretty and I wanted to share it. It's funny how we do that so much in these digital days. How many times have you taken a picture of something pretty for the purpose of sharing it?

This made me think about the importance of sharing our unique stories—more specifically, sharing what God has done for us. Our testimony. Tell your friends. Tell your spouse. If you get a chance to share something that God has done for you, do it. You don't need a crowd or stage.

God wants us to share what He's done for us. In Mark 5:19, after Jesus healed the demon-possessed man, he said, "Go home to your friends, and tell them what great things the Lord has done for you, and how He has had compassion on you." It was a command.

There are reasons for sharing. I wanted to share the photo of the tree because my friends wouldn't experience it otherwise. I want to share what God has done for the same reason. I want to hear others' stories because I don't have the time or desire to experience everything myself. We never know when we present something in a way that will speak to someone when everyone else was unsuccessful. Your voice, your story, your approach might be the ticket.

Sharing our stories increases our faith. I often don't realize how significant something is until I look back on it and choose to share it. It builds my faith and helps build the faith of others. I don't doubt the presence of God in my life because I have seen it. When I tell others, it brings those experiences back to mind. It is a reminder of God's faithfulness. It is a doubt squasher. Have you witnessed answered prayer? Wow. Then share it with others!

We were made for relationships and community. When we share our experiences with others, we help alleviate feelings of being alone. Sometimes knowing that someone else understands is enough. We don't always know when our story is helping someone else, but rest assured there is nothing new under the sun. Someone is connecting with your experiences in a way that God is using to encourage and lift them out of their pit.

Perhaps you're going through a valley before any of your tribe. Your story becomes the light that helps guide them when it's their turn. It's the way-finder sign in their wilderness. It's comforting and strengthening to know that people survive.

Own your story. Words are powerful. Tell the things that God has done for you. Repeat as needed.

Action: Share your story with a friend.

Winds of Change

AND DO NOT BE CONFORMED TO THIS WORLD, BUT BE
TRANSFORMED BY THE RENEWING OF YOUR MIND, THAT
YOU MAY PROVE WHAT IS THAT GOOD AND ACCEPTABLE
AND PERFECT WILL OF GOD.

—ROMANS 12:2

O n one of my walks, a long cloud with a very defined edge got my attention. I don't study cloud shapes often, but it was so distinct that I noticed it and did a double take. Clouds are interesting, and while I'm no meteorologist, I do remember from science lessons there are different types.

Some are fluffy and harmless and make us think of beautiful days. Some are dark and ominous and bring storms. I realized, while looking at the clouds that morning, they looked just like the previous ones several days before, but it wasn't the same. There was one key difference. The air was much cooler.

The breeze blowing those clouds around also brought a twenty-degree difference in temperature. After a string of days in the nineties, the drop to the seventies was a noticeably sharp change. I couldn't see this change. Everything looked the same. But thanks to weather forecasting and good technology, we knew it was coming. There was a time, though, when we wouldn't have known this change was coming, and it would have caught us off guard.

Life is similar. Sometimes we wake up and something has happened to change everything. Maybe our world looks the same but feels different. Sometimes as we age, we start to see things differently. Not all change is bad, but we don't always view it that way. We are often scared of it or unsure that it will make things better.

Occasionally, we look forward to change if we know it's coming or if we know we need it. I never get more excited about that prospect than with a change of scenery, which means I'm getting a vacation.

There aren't many certainties in life, but one is change will come. Sickness and death come. New babies are born. Children grow. Marriages come and go. Jobs end. Friendships can shift. We change our minds. Sometimes a bad situation changes for the better. We can't always control the change, but we can remember that God is the same yesterday, today, and forever.

Ecclesiastes 3 tells us there is a time and purpose for every season. God changes the times and seasons, but He is always with us, regardless of what those seasons bring. We can be assured that if we seek His will, He will take care of us. Romans 12:2 talks about transforming our minds. The definition of transformed refers to "dramatic change." The Message translation refers to God changing us from the inside out.

I don't know about you, but I want God to bring out the best in me. How much better would the world be if we allowed God to bring out the best in us? Focus less on the external variables that lead to change and more on the one who doesn't change. That keeps us from spiraling out of control. It sets our priorities. It gives us hope and something solid to hold on to when the unavoidable outside change comes blowing in.

Action: Make a list of unchanging characteristics of God. Keep it where you can see it.

God Is Good

D o you ever notice that occasionally you can see the moon during the day? During election week in November, as I walked during the mornings, I could see the moon and sun in the sky at the same time, and it became all I could think about. What a good week for that observation.

To sum up the science behind it, we see the moon during the day because its location is the right place to reflect the sun's light enough that it stays brighter than the sky. It's like extra light. Of all weeks, that one, so full of uncertainty and anxiety for many, we sure needed extra light.

It reminded me that the moon has been right there since God put it there, whether we see it or not. I don't know about you, but I take a great deal of comfort in that. The knowledge that God put it in place at creation, and it's the same one we're still looking at today, just blows me away. Not only is it the same one, but God arranged it so that sometimes in a week where our world might seem a little darker, we get extra light. I was astounded by that thought.

Light was the first thing God created (Genesis 1:3), and just like all the things He created, it was good. God is still good, whether we see it or not. God is still good, whether we believe it or not. Let's pause here to say that though God is in ultimate control, we have free will, sin exists, and Satan is real and running rampant. Bad things happen. That fact does not change the goodness of God.

We often use the phrase "God is good" when we're talking about being protected. When God has kept us safe from some unpleasant situation or experience, we proclaim that God is good. It is more than that. God is good in all situations. The scripture (Psalm 34:4) "Oh, taste and see that the Lord is good; Blessed is the man who trusts in Him!" often comes to mind when I think about God being good.

The word *taste* is an interesting choice to me. Taste is not a passive word; it requires action to experience it. Think about God's provision for us every single day. I don't mean only when you believe that God's timing has saved you from disaster or even when God's timing has blessed you with something you dared not dream of. I mean take a sample spoon every day and taste more.

Taste and see how God is good in the tiniest details of your life every single day—when you open your eyes in the morning, when you say a prayer, in a deep breath, or a blue sky, a gentle breeze, a drink of cold water, being told you are loved. Give yourself a chance to experience all of God's goodness, not just in big, marquee events. Make the effort. Take a bite. Taste and see that God is good.

Action: Keep a running list of the ways you see God's goodness.

GRACE FIXES DETACHMENT

"'FOR THIS MY SON WAS DEAD AND IS ALIVE AGAIN; HE
WAS LOST AND IS FOUND.' AND THEY BEGAN TO BE MERRY."

—LUKE 15:24

While walking recently, I came across a doll's arm, and the word *detached* became stuck in my head. Do you ever feel detached? Like you've lost your place? Consider that your priorities might be out of line. Perhaps in the middle of change, loss, busyness, or even in the middle of excitement, you realize something is off. Maybe it's a relationship, your job, your purpose, or just the next right thing. It's a weird feeling. You can't quite put your finger on it; you just know something isn't right.

I've felt like that. It's often an insecurity issue for me that the enemy likes to poke. Most recently, God used the parable of the lost son to help me. The youngest son took his inheritance, squandered it, and found himself starving and taking care of someone's pigs to stay alive. When he came to his senses, he decided to go back home and work for his father. Dad saw him coming and decided to throw a party. He welcomed him with no questions. He hugged and kissed him. He didn't ask questions. He was glad he was alive and back home. Meanwhile, his older brother was upset.

This story often comes up when we talk about returning to God after being away from Him. Certainly, that always applies. But what if we take these approaches and apply them to our relationships with people and not just returning to God? Do we have the guts of the son to swallow our pride, own our mistakes, and go back to where we were loved? Do we have the same kind of unconditional love of that father to offer when someone we love comes back to us? Can we forgive and love without judgment when someone admits they chose poorly?

Or do we get mad like the older brother who stayed? He made better life choices in theory, but he was angry he wasn't being celebrated for doing that. There was no party for doing the right thing. He was jealous. He couldn't see that his blessings came in the form of not suffering and having his needs met. He was detached from the big picture.

All these roads lead to the same place if we can look through the lens of Jesus—the lens of grace. Grace in our mistakes. Grace in our relationships. Grace in decision-making. Grace trumps pride. Grace forgives. Grace sees a bigger picture. Grace celebrates. Grace is the glue that puts us back together when we've become detached.

Is something keeping you detached or giving you that not-quite-right feeling? What's holding you back? Come to your senses and let it go. Trust that God's grace will make it right. When we get past those issues, we begin to heal.

If you're in the position to offer grace, do so. If someone isn't living up to your expectations and you're wondering how much grace you should give, the answer is more. God doesn't run out of grace for us, and that's the example we should follow. It isn't easy, but it's where the blessings are. It's where needs are met, wrongs are righted, and where the lost are found.

Action: Examine your relationships. Give more grace.

THERE IS NO INSTA-FAITH

Wait on the Lord; Be of good courage, And He
shall strengthen your heart; Wait, I say, on the
Lord!

—Psalm 27:14

You know the saying that you shouldn't pray for patience because God will put you in situations that help develop it? Those words were on my heart as I walked. I was reminded that good takes time to develop.

We cheat ourselves by checking out too early and by giving up before allowing God to get us ready. We've conditioned ourselves to the drive-through mentality. If it isn't ready immediately, forget it!

Most good stuff in our lives doesn't work that way. God doesn't work that way. Flowers need time to bloom. Food needs time to grow. Babies need time to learn to walk and talk. An education takes years. The things that mean the most to me—health, love, friendship, faith, and trust, among them—all take time.

We must put in some work and go through some hard days for any potential benefits to pay off. One day of exercise or eating well will not make us fit and healthy. We might think we love someone after one look, but we can't begin to understand the depths of love until we go through some ups and downs. It's unlikely we'll have coffee with someone and immediately become best friends. Relationships are built like houses— one brick at a time. It takes shared experiences, laughter, and tears over an extended period. Such valuable gifts take time and sacrifice to develop. Even if there is an instant connection, a real relationship takes time.

Faith and trust are built the same way. Piece by painstaking piece. Patience is required. Most lasting things won't come with shortcuts and instant versions. We build them. It takes time, and we can't speed it up. There is no insta-faith or insta-trust. Trust and faith in God grow when we look back and see the ways He has been faithful. We will never build them without patience.

God will often slow us down. Jesus's first miracle was when He turned the water into wine (John chapter 2). When His mother said they had no wine, Jesus told her it wasn't His time. I think about Jesus waiting on God's timing. If He had to wait, so will we.

It's not easy to wait for suffering to pass or good things to come. Establishing lasting relationships isn't quick. It's not easy to build faith, trust, and patience because they mean delays and waiting. However, they are rich with reward—like the taste of a perfectly ripened piece of fruit or the utter relief of a friend coming through when you needed her the most. Even better is seeing your faith increase as you see God keep His promises.

You may be tired. Tired of waiting for things to get better. Tired of not knowing. Tired of being hurt. Tired of being anxious. Tired of searching for your purpose, your person, or your tribe of people. We are weary of fighting the same battles and wondering why. We are tired of waiting on God to answer and of feeling like He isn't listening. I don't know how to make it easier, but I know it will be worth the wait.

Action: Hang on. Good stuff takes time.

Don't Lose Heart

I returned from a walk one morning and noticed the spot in the driveway where my husband parks his truck. It was a different color. Lighter. The rest of the driveway had become weathered from rain, sun, and activity.

Most everything holds up better with a little protection. Whether it's driveways or people, having some protection helps. It made me think about the challenges of living through a pandemic. Feelings of helplessness, loss, isolation, and grief, among others, were just hard to handle.

Months into our pandemic situation, I wondered if we could tell where we were sheltered and protected. Psalm 46:1 tells us that God is our refuge in trouble. Refuge literally means something providing shelter—shelter from pursuit, danger, or trouble.

When I began to look closely at my situation through those rugged pandemic months, I saw where my edges had been exposed, but mostly I saw that I had been sheltered. I saw where God protected me—from the little things to the big. For instance, I had bought my kids a small swimming pool for cheap at the end of the previous summer. It was sitting in a box in my garage, while people desperate for things to do at home were finding them sold out everywhere. It was an absolute lifesaver. I had already been home and had work on hold when schools closed, and I then had to orchestrate the schedule of school at home. I'll spare you the full list of examples, but I have them. God sheltered me.

This gives me hope and encouragement for days ahead. It is challenging to imagine how to go forward when normal seems so far away. It is downright exhausting to function in a world dealing with such sustained uncertainty. However, when we focus on seeking God as our refuge, He provides it.

It doesn't mean that we don't catch some stray drops of rain, but if we ask for His help and believe, He will not leave us out to be weathered, beaten up, and broken by the storm. Read on in Psalm chapter 27 to the great nugget that is verse 13. It says, "I would have lost heart, unless I had believed that I would see the goodness of the Lord in the land of the living." I didn't write that, but I could have. We all have ample opportunity to lose heart, be it from a pandemic or something we experience individually. Don't. Choose to believe God's Word instead.

Look back over the last few months. Can you see where He has protected you? Where He has sheltered you from the storm? Oh, precious friend, don't lose heart. Believe in the goodness of the Lord and the shelter He promises to provide. You may not realize just how much He is protecting you right now, but when the storm subsides, you will.

Action: Make a list of ways God has protected you. Read it often. Add to it when needed.

THE LIGHT

IN HIM WAS LIFE, AND THE LIFE WAS THE LIGHT OF MEN.
AND THE LIGHT SHINES IN THE DARKNESS, AND THE
DARKNESS DID NOT COMPREHEND IT.

—JOHN 1:4–5

One late fall day as I was walking in a thick fog, I could only see a few yards in front of me. I noticed a couple of cars coming toward me well in advance because I saw their headlights. I couldn't see the vehicles themselves until they got close. I couldn't help but think that the darker it is, the better we can see the light.

In December 2020, we heard a lot about the Bethlehem Star or Christmas Star that we were supposed to be able to see for the first time in eight hundred years. Technically, it wasn't even a star. It was Jupiter and Saturn aligning so that they appeared as one bright star. It had been eight hundred years since the last occurrence!

I sat quietly in my living room one night and looked at the Christmas tree and an angel lantern sitting nearby. The kids were in bed, my husband was asleep on the couch, and all other lights were off. What a peaceful time that was. What kept going through my head as I sat there was the power of the light. I could almost tangibly feel God's peace settle over me as I gazed at that lantern.

The car lights, the Star of Bethlehem, the peace of those Christmas lights—they all stood out and offered hope in the darkness. It is easy to be caught up in the world's darkness. But that's when light is at its brightest. When the fog is thickest. On those winter days when night comes the earliest and stays the longest. When everything else is dark. There is never a bad time to lean in and look closer at a light that points to Jesus.

Light is the first thing God created after the heavens and the earth. It's that important. It's that essential. There are lots of meanings of light. One that strikes me is the most basic. It is simply "something that makes vision possible."

The Gospel of John offers some explanation. Jesus is the light. In John 8:12, after Jesus saves and forgives the woman caught in adultery, He calls himself the light of the world. When we have Him, we walk in light.

Brokenheartedness, sickness, anger, loneliness, fear, uncertainty, and exhaustion all cast their own shadows that leave us feeling in the dark. Lost. Hopeless. Resigned to despair. But Jesus is the light that eclipses the darkness.

Chase the light. Walk in the light and pass it on. Matthew 5:16 tells us to let our light shine before others. How bright our lights can be to others who are lost in the dark. Even if you feel yours has dimmed, you can still shine enough to push back darkness. When your light is reflecting the source of light, darkness is overtaken.

No matter how foggy the morning, how short the day, how dark the season, or heavy the year, the light of Jesus is always shining. He chases the darkness away and makes life possible.

Action: Look for the light. Make a list of places you see it.

Winter

CONSISTENCY IS KEY

AND YOU WILL SEEK ME AND FIND ME, WHEN YOU SEARCH
FOR ME WITH ALL YOUR HEART.

—JEREMIAH 29:13

I do my best thinking when I'm taking my morning walks. Or could it be that I do my best listening then? Some winter days when I'm facing the right direction, an extra cold wind will whip across my face, make my eyes water, and nearly take my breath away. For a split second, I wonder why I keep walking when it is cold.

It is in that moment, that split second, when I can feel the answer in my bones. A voice, not audible but not my own, says, "You don't give yourself a chance to not do it." Whatever the source, it is accurate.

I plan and prepare to walk. I schedule it. I do have some limits. Weather extremes, a sick kid, or an appointment sometimes get in the way. Ultimately, my walks are important to me, so I make time for them. If I waited for perfect conditions, the benefits of my walks wouldn't be nearly as effective. Consistency is the key.

If we only exercise on great days or eat healthy food on occasion, we can't be surprised when we don't feel well or don't lose weight. If we only play a sport or an instrument during actual practice, we are not going to become great. If we always bail out on the plans we make, the invitations will quit coming. Consistency matters.

It matters to our mental and spiritual lives as well. If we think negatively for long enough, we see the world negatively. If we train ourselves to habitually look for the positive, we can see that too.

Jeremiah says seek Him with all your heart. If we consistently spend time seeking God, we will find Him.

When we consistently pray, we will have answers. Regularly reading the Word of God helps us know and understand it better. You don't have to go to church every Sunday to be a Christian, but consistently worshipping and praising with other believers will help make you a better one.

In 1 Corinthians 15:58, Paul said to be steadfast, immovable, always abounding in the work of the Lord. Not just when it's sunny or convenient. Are we being steadfast, unwavering, and consistent in our relationship with God? Do we care enough to make that relationship as important as all others? Are we consistent when conditions are not perfect?

It is hard to anchor in and be immovable in our faith. Satan is trying to trip us up. But if we want to see positive results in anything—our physical shape, our skill at a task, our attitude, or our walk with Christ—consistency is key. We must keep at it on challenging days and around challenging people. We must prioritize consistency.

Don't be surprised if being consistent takes all your heart. God promises we will not labor in vain. Praying, reading scripture, listening for His voice, obeying, and sometimes being still are always worth it. Consistency will gradually make it easier. Consistently live for Jesus, and watch the difference it will make in your life.

Action: Pick a spiritual task that you're not being consistent with and make it a priority.

Don't Quit

But as for you, be strong and do not give up, for
your work will be rewarded.

—2 Chronicles 15:7

One winter day when I chose to walk though not wanting to, I noticed a distinct line in the sky where one side was blue and the other dark. The sun was just about to break through. My perseverance was about to be rewarded with sunshine. It came out. The rest of my walk, while still cold, was with a bright blue, sunshiny sky.

That day, I had almost let snowflakes throw me off and keep me inside. I'm glad I didn't. It turned out to be a perfectly fine day for walking, and God put something on my heart. I love it when He does that. His message was "Don't give up when it looks hard. Don't quit when it is hard." We don't know just how close breakthrough might be. The clearing might be steps away.

I know what you're thinking. *You don't understand how hard it is. You don't know what I'm going through. You don't know how long I've been hanging on.* I understand because I've had those thoughts too. You're not alone. We all have hard stretches when sometimes life seems too heavy.

As I started running the back stretch toward home, I thought about how strong my legs had become. The consistency of walking daily for the last few years means I can now feel the muscle even when I'm at rest. I thought about that strength and how I knew it was enough. Those thoughts also distracted me from my breathing, which is hard in the cold. I focused on my strength, not my weakness.

It is easier to keep going when you're focused on where your strength is coming from. I don't run long distances, but I have gone through stretches of life that required endurance. Life requires endurance. Grief, pain, brokenness, busyness, uncertainty, it all puts us in a similar spot. We focus on where it hurts and want to quit. We want the hard to end.

Dear friend, let me remind you where your strength comes from. Isaiah 41:10 says God will strengthen us. He will uphold us. God will not wear out. He will not let you down. He will not leave. He will not let go. He will not forget you. He will reward your endurance. He will make it worth your while to hang on and to finish the race.

In the middle of what is hard, tapping into His strength will pull you through. Don't give up. Keep going when you don't want to. His strength is enough. Clouds will break, and the sun will shine again. Your walk through the valley will end. It has been my experience that the personal strength you gain from each hard season helps you build endurance for the next.

You can do it. You can make it. Don't give up before the breakthrough comes. You are building your strength. You are inspiring others. You are earning the rest and reward that God has promised.

Action: Keep going.

How Are You Carrying It?

For He shall give His angels charge over you, To keep you in all your ways. They shall bear you up in their hands, Lest you dash your foot against a stone.

—Psalm 91:11–12

My husband and sons were on a guys' trip. I miss them when they're gone, but I enjoy having some me time. We all need me time sometimes. It's a reset that lets you get a deep breath.

As part of my reset, I treated myself to a massage. I don't get them regularly, but I've had plenty of them. That was a good one, as I asked for focus on my feet and legs because of the walking I do. Afterward, the massage therapist asked how much I walk and then said, "I can tell."

He said from his perspective, I didn't have any other issues. I was in good shape. I could have told him that. The next day, as I was getting ready for church by putting on leggings, I thought about the whole conversation again.

I had just gone through a season of loss that could have left me carrying around stress and tension that might show up in my muscles. Death of close loved ones can do that. It wouldn't have been surprising if my tension was tangible. It wasn't. It's because of how I carried it. Or rather who helped me carry it. How are you carrying your stressors? Are you letting God help you?

It made me think of that meme that says, "Just because I carry it well doesn't mean it isn't heavy." It was heavy. Friends, it's God who did the heavy lifting. When God is doing the carrying, we don't have to be in knots. We can come through it. Even when it doesn't make sense and when the whole world would understand if we were knotted up in tension. He will carry us all the way through.

The book of Isaiah is full of reminders of how God is with us, strengthens us, upholds us, helps us, carries us. Isaiah 46:4 says He will carry us and deliver us.

He promises to see us through. Sometimes He gives us direction, and other times He carries us. If we focus on not fighting Him, we might even come out better. If we fight Him like a toddler fighting against being carried out of a candy store, then we might get some self-inflicted bumps and bruises!

I don't know what heavy, stressful stuff you've been going through, but stop and look at how you're carrying it. Give it to God, and let Him do your heavy lifting. Let Him carry you without a fight. Take the help He provides. Just hang on tight and let Him be God.

I won't promise that you'll always get through it unscathed, but He can make great use of bumps and bruises. These serve as a reminder, a lesson, a guide for the future, both to us and to the many people who witness our lives. However, I will promise, because God promises, that He will carry you through.

Action: What's weighing heavy on you today? Ask God to help you carry it.

SEEING CLEARLY

FOR OUR LIGHT AFFLICTION, WHICH IS BUT FOR A MOMENT,
IS WORKING FOR US A FAR MORE EXCEEDING AND ETERNAL
WEIGHT OF GLORY, WHILE WE DO NOT LOOK AT THE THINGS
WHICH ARE SEEN, BUT AT THE THINGS WHICH ARE NOT
SEEN. FOR THE THINGS WHICH ARE SEEN ARE TEMPORARY,
BUT THE THINGS WHICH ARE NOT SEEN ARE ETERNAL.

—2 CORINTHIANS 4:17–18

We all know how much fun it is to visit the dentist, and I must share that I had the pleasure of doing that this week! I had to put on the protective glasses to keep the spray from getting in my eyes. The hygienist apologized for how cloudy and scratched up they were after repeated cleanings. The room immediately seemed fuzzy when I put them on.

Once she was done and I took off the glasses, I got up to rinse with mouthwash at the sink. As I looked in that mirror, I could see some gray hairs and the crow's feet at the corners of my eyes. I turned and asked her if I could please have those glasses back because then I wouldn't be able to see the gray and the wrinkles. We shared a laugh about it.

Those cloudy glasses remind me that life is often how we see it. Where we're looking and our perspective make a difference in how our days go. Is your world scuffed up and cloudy? Are you seeing things the way you should?

I thought about those glasses as I walked. I noticed one certain tree along my path. It looks just like many trees do in the winter. Gray background, mostly empty branches just standing firm through the winter. Since I walk that same route all the time, I know something else about that tree. In the summer, when it's in full bloom, it is shaped like a heart. It makes me happy every time I see it. On the cold gray days of winter, I can still see the heart.

It was approximately twenty-five degrees as I walked by that tree the day after the dentist visit. I could see my breath, and my fingers were stinging cold. I thought of that heart shape. And summer. And blue skies. And warmth. I was thankful that I could see beyond today.

In 2 Corinthians 4:17–18, Paul writes that our struggles are temporary. We don't want to focus too much on our present circumstances because it all changes. We might need to take off our scuffed-up earthly glasses so we can fix our gaze on what is unseen. When I look at that tree in the cold of winter, I see what is unseen. I don't want anything to cloud my view of God and how much He loves all of us.

We need to look beyond the temporary. That barren tree is full of life. It will show its heart again on warmer days. That helps me see past temporary circumstances to the everlasting love that God has for us. I see how He keeps His promises. I see how He is just as faithful on winter days as He is on summer days.

Action: Is your view of God scuffed up? Take off those earthly glasses and look again.

STANDING IN THE SUN

TRULY THE LIGHT IS SWEET, AND IT IS PLEASANT FOR THE
EYES TO BEHOLD THE SUN.

—ECCLESIASTES 11:7

When I walk on super cold days, I often stay cold all day. My thermostat stays set on seventy-two, but some days I still freeze. One day, I poured a mug of coffee, mostly just to hold. Then I went to the back door and stood there in the sunlight, searching for warmth.

I turned like I was on a BBQ spit. I don't know how long I stood there but long enough to drink my coffee. I felt I shouldn't just stand there and shut my brain off, so I used it as quiet time with God.

He led my thoughts to a simple place: we should stand in the sun more. Sunshine is a big deal that we take for granted. We wouldn't be here without it. We need to seek out and hold on to the sunshine in our lives. That might be in the form of actual rays of sun, people who feel like sunshine to us, or a place or memory. Sometimes we are the sunshine for others.

You've probably seen that quote "If you can't find the sunshine, be the sunshine," but have you put it into practice? When someone is going through dark days and really needs some light, have you been sunshine for them? It is easy. You can pray for someone, check on them, tell them you love or appreciate them.

As I stood warming in my patch of afternoon sunlight, I thought about how I needed sunlight from others. I receive it when a friend helps me with technology issues, through encouraging words, time spent, and just providing laughter.

My gaze shifted to a picture of a sunrise over the house and ridge where I grew up. Sunny days and happy times flooded my memories. That photo reminded me of the warmth of a good childhood. Then I looked down at the rocking chair that sits below that picture. It was my mom's. I broke it while throwing a temper tantrum as a child. Mom gifted the damaged chair to me when she died as a reminder to make better choices. It could just be broken and worthless, but to me it's sunshine and priceless because it reminds me of Mom.

Sometimes we must look harder to find the sun. It's worth seeking though. Just like it is worth seeking God. It's worth standing in that light for a few minutes to warm yourself. At times, you need to warm your hands, and other times, you need to warm your heart. We need to seek God and stand in the knowledge of His warmth and comfort, for if we do, He'll provide sun. Other days, we need to share Him with others. People are seeking anything that might help. Make sure you're encouraging people to seek His light. That's an unshakable warmth.

Action: Find a way to be sunshine for someone today. When you share sunshine with others, you can't keep it from yourself.

WHEN YOUR HEAD IS DOWN

One winter morning, I took my usual walk in blustery, snowy conditions. According to Google, the temperature when I left my house that day was thirty-two degrees with a "feels like" temperature of twenty-five thanks to the wind conditions. The wind was blowing and swirling the snow.

For several stretches of the three-mile journey that day, the snowflakes were whipping right into my face. It stung a little, so I had to put my head down and watch one step at a time. Most of that walk looked the same—like blacktop and tennis shoes. I didn't pass a single other walker on the way. Can't imagine why!

God reminded me that sometimes our journey is warm and sunny, dotted with colorful flowers and full of neighbors and walkers ready to speak or wave. Sometimes it requires putting our head down and focusing on the step right in front of us. Friends, if you're in a head-down season, keep going. It's only a piece of the journey, not the whole thing.

There are two key points that we need to remember when we're in a hard season that requires all our attention to be right on the hard step in front of us. The first is that we never have to be alone. Psalm 16:8 tells us that when we set the Lord before us, He stays right beside us all the time. He doesn't leave when blustery winds whip snow in our faces. We may feel alone and only see the tops of our own tennis shoes, but He goes with us into the head-down season.

The second key point worthy of focus is that the journey has an end. Hard, head-down seasons are an absolute certainty in earthly life, but they are temporary. Isaiah 43:1–3 offers a great perspective on this truth.

"But now, thus says the Lord, who created you, O Jacob, And He who formed you, O Israel: 'Fear not for I have redeemed you; I have called you by your name; You are Mine. When you pass through the waters, I will be with you; And through the rivers, they shall not overflow you. When you walk through the fire, you shall not be burned, Nor shall the flame scorch you. For I am the Lord your God, the Holy One of Israel, your Savior; I gave Egypt for your ransom, Ethiopia and Seba in your place.'"

Friends, I want us to linger on the phrase "when you walk through" for just a bit. Head-down seasons are a *when*, not an *if*. But my absolute favorite part is the word *through*. You can and will come through your hard season when you set the Lord before you. There is no reason to fear the cold, the wind, the snow, the rivers, the fires, or whatever the enemy can throw at us. We don't have to stop or get stuck in the middle. God makes the way through.

Action: If you're in a head-down season, go ahead, pray, and then keep walking.

What We Get Used To

That you put off, concerning your former conduct,
the old man which grows corrupt according to
the deceitful lusts.

—Ephesians 4:22

One winter day as I went for my morning walk, it was forty-one degrees. That's not exactly warm, but I barely needed my jacket because I had gotten so used to twenty-degree weather. The next day, it was back to twenty-four degrees.

Isn't it funny how the same temperature can be warm or cold, depending on what we've gotten used to? When the early spring temperature climbs to sixty, my children believe they should break out the shorts. Sixty degrees feels much warmer when our bodies have acclimated to thirty or forty degrees. The flip side is true in the fall as well. That first sixty-degree day has us running for the sweaters and the pumpkin spice.

I wonder how many other parts of life I've grown hot or cold to simply because I've gotten used to them. Have I started to accept things I shouldn't just because I've gotten used to something? Friends, reality doesn't change just because we've acclimated to a certain way. I still needed a coat on that forty-one-degree morning even though it was twenty degrees warmer than every other day that week. Being used to colder temperatures didn't make forty-one degrees a warm day; it just felt that way.

This mentality fuels complacency in our spiritual lives if we're not careful. Have you ever gotten out of the habit of going to church? Perhaps you slowly slipped out of having regular prayer time, and now you hardly even notice. Even worse, maybe you've been in a season where you've loosened your standards on sin bit by bit, until you look up and realize that you've crossed a line you should never have crossed.

Has your heart grown hard over time because you have become used to the way you were treated or the way it has always been? We don't have to accept what we've grown used to. Ephesians 4:17–24 is a passage that talks about becoming new after we have hardened our hearts and grown corrupt. Verses 23–24 say, "And be renewed in the spirit of your mind, and that you put on the new man which was created according to God, in righteousness and true holiness."

We don't wake up suddenly to find ourselves in a place we shouldn't be. It happens over time when we begin to get used to what gradually becomes acceptable. What God deems as wrong doesn't become right because we've learned to accept it. God is still speaking even if we've grown accustomed to not listening. We shouldn't abandon loving one another because some people don't love us.

Don't get complacent just because you've learned how to tolerate the cold or to accept less. Friends, this is a good day to renew your mind and resume being who God created you to be.

Action: Be honest with yourself and determine where you've slipped into complacency. Ask God to help you renew your mind in those areas.

BLACK ICE

SO THEN FAITH COMES BY HEARING, AND HEARING BY THE WORD OF GOD.

—ROMANS 10:17

It would have been a great day to choose not to walk, but I was stubborn and walked anyway. I nearly wiped out on black ice about three times.

From a distance, the road looked fine, but once I started walking, I could feel the slickness and some crunching of ice under my feet. You know what happens when you start walking on ice? You slow down. You can't take full strides and walk normally. On that walk, I had to slow down and mind my steps closely. First, I tried to avoid the ice, and then I had to be careful walking on it when it couldn't be avoided.

It made me think about how we walk through life with so many voices vying for our attention and claiming to have all the answers. Some of those voices are as slippery and dangerous as black ice. We must slow down and mind our steps. It's crucial that we be careful of the voices we listen to, the people we surround ourselves with, and the steps we take.

It's discernment that we need on this journey fraught with black ice and hidden danger. At its most basic, discernment means being able to tell the difference between true and false. Most of us want to practice that discernment so we make the correct steps. We don't want to rush into a dangerous spot that causes us to stumble and fall.

Just like physically walking on ice, we need to deliberately slow down. That's not easy in today's world, but it is necessary. If we're constantly racing through life without pausing to listen for God's guidance, then we're bound to hit some slick spots and potentially wipe out.

Listening for God can be its own challenge. He doesn't usually offer the loud and clear, audible response or even the neon sign that we're often wishing for. That's not to say He won't or can't but that we usually must pay closer attention to hear His voice. We need to be a little closer and quieter when we're listening for God.

In 1 Kings chapter 19, God came to Elijah in a "still small voice." He wasn't in the loud or flashy wind, earthquake, or fire. He was in the quiet. He's in the small, careful, deliberate steps.

Another way we can learn to hear and to discern is by reading the Word. Romans 10:17 says, "So then faith comes by hearing, and hearing by the word of God."

Hearing comes by the Word. We begin to know God's voice when we read the words that He gave to us. We learn about who He is, His character, His way. Just like any relationship, when we spend time with Him and learn about Him, we begin to learn His voice. We can better discern it from all the white noise of other voices. That, in turn, helps us avoid those patches of danger that can be so difficult to see. Slow down, listen, and get home safely.

Action: Devote regular time to reading the Bible and then quietly listen for God's voice in your life.

Enduring Winter

Bears all things, believes all things, hopes all things, endures all things.

—1 Corinthians 13:7

Walking outside in the winter sometimes means I must decide if I'm willing to walk in the rain. I don't particularly enjoy that, especially on winter days. It makes it extra cold. My clothes get wet. Worse yet, my shoes and socks get wet.

One February day, despite the rain, I went out anyway, and I even reached a milestone on the app that tracks my distance. I passed one hundred kilometers for the year, which is about sixty-five miles. That was sixty-five miles of January and February walking. It was not always ideal conditions. But as I got back to my house, I noticed something special. There were buds on the tree in my front yard.

On a cold, rainy winter day, that absolutely flooded my soul with hope. In the middle of the gray and drizzle, I was reminded that winter never lasts forever. Believe me, I know it can feel like it.

This rainy walk was one year after the doctor told my dad there was nothing else they could do for him. For a year, I was actively dealing with my father's death—preparing for it, watching it happen, and then wrapping up his life. It felt like winter for a long time. There's nothing unique to my story. We all must go through seasons of suffering that feel like the deepest, unending winter. We just have to endure, but winter always ends.

Most of us are familiar with 1 Corinthians 13 (the love chapter). Verse 7 points out that love "endures all things," and it always gives me pause. Endure means to suffer patiently. Part of love is suffering patiently. I suffer through winter patiently. I endure it.

I think about enduring that hard year. I loved my dad, so I endured what I had to. You, too, may have endured suffering because you loved someone. The Bible tells us to rejoice in our sufferings because they produce hope (Romans 5:3–5). They make us who God wants us to be. Those are hard words to read.

Does that mean I have to rejoice in wintertime? You may choose to disagree, but I think it does. I have to work really hard to rejoice in the day the Lord has made when I'm walking in cold rain. When it's super rainy, I often say it's a good day for ducks because I heard my dad say it many times. It reminds me that we need both rain and sun. We need the winter, whether I like it or not. Many people might benefit from circumstances I don't appreciate or understand. We need a little bit of suffering because there's tremendous value in it.

When we can endure it all the way through, we'll see that suffering ends in hope. Winter ends. The sun shines again. The suffering might change us, but it's so worth it to hang on.

If I could follow you around all day, clap, and shout encouragement for you, I would. Instead, I can tell you to notice God's creation. Never mind winter; look for the buds of spring. Look for the hope. Look for God. He's always there.

Action: Make it a point to look for something today that makes you hopeful.

AT THE TOP

HAVING THEN GIFTS DIFFERING ACCORDING TO THE GRACE
THAT IS GIVEN TO US, LET US USE THEM: IF PROPHECY, LET
US PROPHESY IN PROPORTION TO OUR FAITH; OR MINISTRY,
LET US USE IT IN OUR MINISTERING; HE WHO TEACHES,
IN TEACHING; HE WHO EXHORTS, IN EXHORTATION; HE
WHO GIVES, WITH LIBERALITY; HE WHO LEADS, WITH
DILIGENCE; HE WHO SHOWS MERCY, WITH CHEERFULNESS.

—ROMANS 12:6–8

While I walked one morning, I saw a squirrel sitting on the very top of a tree branch that had been trimmed off. My first thought was, *Now that it's at the top, what happens next?* No sooner had that thought popped in my head than I noticed a bird sitting at the top of another branch in the same tree.

They were at about the same height in the tree, but there was a key difference. The squirrel was maxed out. It was as far up as it could go. Meanwhile, the bird was barely beginning. It was just a rest stop for the bird. At the same spot, one had reached its peak, and the other was just getting started.

People are similar. Your goals, abilities, and peaks are not mine. Mine are not yours. Stop comparing yourself to the creature two branches over. The popular phrase "stay in your lane" comes to mind.

Those verses in Romans are clear. They draw out some boundaries, and isn't that what it means to stay in our lane? Observe the boundaries. God gave us different dreams, different skills, and different lanes on purpose. It's OK not to be in the same place as someone else. Our journeys are not the same. God didn't put us all on the same road. Comparing yourself with someone on a different road with a different car or bike or feet is worthless.

We need to run our own race and stay in our own lane. If God gave us wings, He's probably not going to ask us to swim. He gave us different gifts and abilities for the betterment of all. If we get so distracted and focused on what's happening in other lanes, we veer off course and cause all sorts of problems we may not be able to come back from.

A good example of this is found in John 12:1–8. Mary was using expensive oil to anoint Jesus's feet. She was doing what she felt called to do. Judas, of all people, took exception and said they should sell the oil and give the money to the poor. Except Judas didn't care about the poor; rather, he just happened to have the money box and was stealing off the top. He was way out of his lane and trying to derail others from their own path. Judas had become completely undone by focusing outside his lane.

If that squirrel tried to be a bird, it wouldn't go well. Just as if we focus more on the races other people are running, it's going to hurt our own race. Stay in your lane.

Action: If you have time to look outside your lane, just clap for those who are doing well in theirs.

THE STRUGGLE IS NEEDED

A blue jay caught my attention while I was walking this morning. I saw it moving from one branch to another in a tree. I noticed it because the leaves were off the tree, and the sky was gray. I thought about that as I continued, and I began to see more brightly colored birds. Those blue jays and cardinals would be much tougher to see in the summer when the trees are full, the sky is blue, and color abounds. In the starkness of a winter landscape, those feathered friends stood out. I could see them at a distance.

Seeing God is kind of the same thing. We often don't look and see Him when everything is in full bloom and life is going the way we want. When everything is going as we want it, we are often guilty of not looking further. Instead, we look for Him when the leaves fall and struggle comes. Sometimes, when it's winter, when it's a dark season, we just need to open our eyes, and He is more easily seen.

James 1:17 reminds us that with God, there is no variation. He doesn't change when the seasons or circumstances change. We can count on Him to be with us always.

Look for the Lord in the dark days of winter, of grief, of bitterness, of sickness, of madness, of uncertainty. He will show you that He's still there and is undaunted by the circumstances of the day.

The good news is made even better when we realize there is more than just knowing He is there. He wants us to experience Him and the help He provides. Hebrews 4:16 says, "Let us therefore come boldly to the throne of grace, that we may obtain mercy and find grace to help in time of need."

The Lord desires that we come to Him in all the days and seasons. We must face days where we are desperate for help so that we ask and receive. When we confidently approach God in the dark, cold days of winter, the mercy and grace that He freely gives stand out in our lives, just like those colorful birds. We can more easily see the help He is giving, even from a distance, when everything doesn't look the way we think it should.

God is not distant from us unless we distance ourselves from Him. He goes before us. He goes with us. And He never forsakes or leaves us, so we don't need to fear the struggles because we can count on Him (Deuteronomy 31:8).

Let's boldly seek God out in the hardest of the hard days and allow Him to show up and provide the help we need, as only He can. Against the backdrop of need, God's grace is seen all the better.

Action: Boldly seek God today and ask Him to show up in your struggle.

One Step at a Time

"Give us day by day our daily bread."

—Luke 11:3

As I was logging my daily miles one morning, I thought about my poor walking shoes. They were very nearly worn out. It was no wonder, as according to the app I use to track my mileage, I had put about four hundred miles on that pair of shoes. That's a lot of miles. It was time to get another pair.

But I had them all worn in, just as I like them, and I don't like breaking in a new pair. They looked OK if I was looking down at the tops of them. If you saw me walking in them, they looked fine. However, if you flipped them over and looked at the bottoms, you'd see they were about to wear away. If you looked inside them, you would see that I had worn holes in them.

Taking one step at a time, I had walked four hundred miles. I thought about that for a bit, and then my mind drifted back to some conversations I had with people in the days prior. The theme of those chats was telling others that I was putting one foot in front of the other.

It was my way of saying that I just keep on going. I was still dealing with the grief of losing my dad. Maybe more than dealing with grief, I was still working my way through closing the estate, which is a long, tiring, emotional journey. The best way I know to describe it is just putting one foot in front of the other and keep doing the next thing.

I felt a bit like my walking shoes. I was worn down from the marathon of walking a grief-ridden gauntlet. Most of the time, I was fine and functional. On those days, I suspect multiple people were praying for me, so I did well. Then other days, I felt like pieces of me had worn off on the road. I found myself praying that there was enough of me left to finish walking through that season.

I try to stay in a mindset of "give us this day our daily bread." I don't know what tomorrow holds, but I do know God is taking care of me today. I trust He will do the same tomorrow. I know I must focus on putting one foot in front of the other every day. I hope you can find it helpful too. Walk with me, and let's take the next step.

You can go a long way just by putting one foot in front of the other. Like my old shoes, I think maybe we get worn in just the right way during the process. Now, I'm a little more empathetic and sympathetic to others. I am probably stronger today than I was six months ago or have ever been. I'm a lot more receptive to God and, I hope, much closer to being the person He wants me to be. It's funny how life's battles can do that to you.

If you are tired and struggling today, I get it. Me too. Come on and start the journey. We are going to come out better than we went in. We are going to make it one step at a time.

Action: Just do what needs to be done next.

Thousand-Mile Journey

He has shown you, O man, what is good; And what does the Lord require of you But to do justly, To love mercy, And to walk humbly with your God?

—Micah 6:8

The journey of a thousand miles begins with a single step. I dare say we've all heard that quote, which is attributed to Chinese philosopher Lao Tzu. It's hard to argue with those words. Those first steps get attention. They're exciting and sometimes a little scary. We're often prepared and pumped for that first step. The thing about that thousand-mile journey, though, is that it takes a whole lot of steps.

I have firsthand experience with this. I deliberately saved this devotional for the end of the book, which was inspired by my personal steps. I set a goal to walk one thousand miles in a year. I did it. And shortly after I completed that goal, this book began to take shape.

I can report that the journey of a thousand miles also ends with a single step. The real work is done in between that first and that last step. Step after step after step on the days when it's swelteringly hot, blustery cold, rainy, or thick with pollen. When your hip hurts or there are blisters on your feet. When you remember that it's optional and no one is making you do it. I learned that our best work is just continuing to walk when it would be easier to stop.

Friends, my daily walks are a metaphor for much of life, especially a Christian life. We have no choice about when we are born, but we do get to choose about being born again—about choosing to walk with God. Over and over, God promises to save, love, forgive, rescue, and protect us; to offer us grace and never leave or forsake us, no matter where or how far our journey takes us. He is there with us every step. He never fails us. We are only required to choose and obey Him.

Micah 6:8 says, "He has shown you, O man, what is good; And what does the Lord require of you But to do justly, To love mercy, And to walk humbly with your God?" Walking with God is not always an easy task, but it is always worthwhile. The more you truly walk with Him, the more you desire to walk with Him.

Life journeys are guaranteed to include suffering. God has made no secret of that. We can expect conditions to be less than ideal. We can expect some pain. There are high odds that we will have to do much of it alone, with no audience to cheer us on. Satan will heckle us and try to get us to quit. Some days, we really must seek God to know He is there. But as we begin to find Him more frequently and realize just how close He is, we learn that our heart desires Him more and more.

From the first step to the last step, there is no journey more rewarding than walking with the Lord.

Action: Take a walk. Ask God to go with you.